Cultivating a
Cutting-Edge
Children's Church

Published by Morning Joy Media.

Visit www.morningjoymedia.com for more information on bulk discounts and special promotions, or e-mail your questions to info@morningjoymedia.com.

Cover Design: Timothy Gruber
Interior Design: Debbie Capeci

Cataloging-In-Publication Data

Gruber, Dick.
 Cultivating a Cutting-Edge Children's Church / by Dick Gruber ;
 p. cm.
 Summary: Children's ministry expert Dick Gruber details proven methods for children's church workers to provide a service for children that ministers to the whole child: physical, spiritual, mental, and social.

ISBN 978-1-937107-16-1 (pbk.)

Subjects:
 1. Church work with children. 2. Christian education of children. I. Title.

Printed in the United States of America

Cultivating a
Cutting-Edge
Children's Church

Dick Gruber

Morning Joy Media
Spring City, Pennsylvania

why read this book?

KNOWLEDGE

It is my prayer that you will learn more about the ministry of children's church through this book.

INSPIRATION

I trust that God will bless you, challenge your philosophy of ministry, and inspire you to make children's church a service that can benefit every child for eternity.

DECISION

Above all, decide now that you will open your heart and mind to what God has for you and your children. Choose this day whom you will serve.

contact Dick Gruber

E-mail address: dagruber@vfcc.edu

Web addresses:

www.dickgruber.com

www.cmuo.com

www.childrensministrytalk.com

Office address:

Valley Forge Christian College

1401 Charlestown Road

Phoenixville, PA 19460

contents

how gruber got into children's church

My fiancée, Darlene, and I followed the children down the rusty bus steps, across the parking lot, and into the church. For several weeks we had been helping as song leaders on a church bus. (At that time we didn't know this was called *ministry*. We just wanted to serve God any way we could.) But this Sunday we were headed for the sanctuary.

It seemed an ordinary enough morning that Sunday in the spring of 1975. People attended Sunday school, walked their dogs, slept in, and yelled at their children. The sky was overcast and the snow melted enough to birth hopes of coming green. But in looking back, I see the significance that Sunday played in the revelation of God's plan for me, my wife to be, the children we would have at home and church, and children's church leaders around the globe.

Dick and Darlene, circa 1979

The children pushed their way up the stairs, through the doors, and into the sanctuary. Seating was found amidst giggles, wonderment, and a few choruses being played on the grand piano. Mrs. Walker stood and opened in prayer. That prayer opened a service, but more than that, it introduced me to the world of children's church.

Oh, I had visited once before. It was an accident really. Or perhaps it was one of those amusing, amazing times when God steps into the life of one of his children. My first Sunday at Glad Tidings Church had found me arriving early, finding a seat in the balcony, and witnessing my first children's church service. I was amazed as children enjoyed worship, preaching of the Word at their own level, and a time of prayer. "This is for me," I decided that day. When the time was right and the opportunity offered, I became an official helper.

My first day as a children's church helper was uneventful. I don't remember the message preached or the songs sung. I do recall the presence of God and the joy of being part of an important ministry in the church. God, in his infinite wisdom, had placed me in a children's church.

For almost a year and a half, Darlene and I served in that bus ministry and children's church. Eventually the leader even allowed us to minister up front. During that year we were married, had our first child, and learned how to operate a puppet. God is so good!

Since that rather ordinary beginning, we have served in seven churches in five states. Each church has introduced us to new opportunities, traditions, and friends. Our four children were born in four different states.

The children's churches that Darlene and I have served in over the years have varied in numbers and styles. In one church we had 12 children each Sunday, in another over 250. In Farmington, Minnesota, we ministered to a group that ranged from 50 to 120 as the church grew. Our numbers have varied depending on weather, holidays, and the usher's abilities to count children and puppets. The highest single attendance on a Sunday morning was 317 on Easter Sunday one year. That was at the People's Church in Salem, Oregon.

We have served a variety of age groupings depending on the senior pastor's vision for children's church. In one case, that vision was driven by the pastor's need to get his four-year-old son out of the main sanctuary. So we gladly ministered to four- through twelve-year-old children. In another church we had kindergarten through grade six. In yet another congregation we served fourth, fifth, and sixth graders in one room. We even served in a church where we were able to divide up the children's church into two groups: kindergarten through second grade, and third through sixth grade.

I have written this brief history of our children's church ministry so that you might know I am an ordinary children's church leader. I have acquired a formal education over the years, but a far deeper education has been wrought as I have cried with, prayed for, and ministered to his little children and those that serve them.

Dick as a clown with son Aaron

Names such as Jerry Strandquist, Dan Hines, Elaine Walker, Dan Rector, Bob Hahn, Jim Wideman, Ed Corbin, George Edgerly and Todd Beranak will forever be locked in my memory as contributors to the Dick Gruber that writes this book. More than to the support of these good friends and mentors, I must give credit to the children: the children of Eden Prairie, Farmington, and Bloomington, Minnesota; Salem, Oregon; Springfield, Missouri; and Royersford, Pennsylvania. Credit and heartfelt thanks must go to those children who have lived in my home, teaching me daily what a good children's church leader should be and how he should live. Sarah, Aaron, Rachel, and Timothy have defined and redefined my understanding of worship, attention span, and ministry.

Finally, I salute my wife, Darlene. We began in this ministry before we were married. She has served by my side faithfully all of these years. Darlene is as much a children's pastor as I. She has mentored me in the important aspects of ministry: relationships, empathy, and godliness. Her support and editorial skills have contributed greatly to this work.

I am Dick Gruber, an ordinary children's church worker. I have been a volunteer, paid pastor, helper, leader, husband, and father. I am a children's church leader sharing with you, another children's church leader. My prayer is that you will enjoy and benefit from this work. My trust is that God will use this tool to assist you in evaluating and improving your children's church.

the cutting-edge children's church

We cannot look at the components of a cutting-edge children's church in isolation. We must explore the cutting-edge children's pastor hand in hand with his church time, for any and every right decision concerning the style and format of children's church will flow from the children's pastor's life.

WHAT IS CUTTING EDGE, REALLY?

Oftentimes, pastors call me when they begin looking for a children's pastor. In recent years, those searching for a children's pastor have described their dream person as someone that is "cutting edge." When I question the prospective pastor as to what he means, I get all kinds of answers. Some of the words used to describe the "cutting-edge" children's pastor are young, exciting, entertaining, techno-savvy, and full of energy.

Let me describe a cutting-edge children's pastor to you. This person can be young or old. I know "sharp" ministers of all ages. The idea that a young person will automatically be a cutting-edge person is ludicrous. There are some very well-trained, well-rounded children's pastors coming out of our colleges that have made this ministry a priority. But, some of the most forward-thinking and creative children's pastors in America are over forty years of age. Many of our older children's pastors have a great deal of wisdom, experience in administration, and a relational ministry with the children and their families.

I have met some fine cutting-edge children's workers who haven't reached twenty-five years of age. I find others to be nothing more than good entertainers. But pastoring children includes much more than running a fun children's church. Cutting-edge children's pastors will build relationships with children and families. They will love and listen to children in and out of church. They will visit homes, hospitals, PTA meetings, recitals, and ball games. They will counsel, equip, and care for children, families, and those who work with the kids.

NON-NEGOTIABLE!

First and foremost, a cutting-edge children's pastor must be a person who has spent time developing an intimate relationship with Christ. There is no greater task assigned to the children's leader than that of getting to know Christ through regular Bible study, prayer, and times of solitude. If Jesus needed to go out to quiet places and spend time with God, how much more does the children's church leader? Reggie McNeal writes, "Great spiritual leaders are great spiritual leaders because they enjoy exceptional communion with God. Failure to establish intimacy with the Almighty imposes a limit on genuine spiritual leadership."[1] If you seek to be truly cutting edge, then spend time with Jesus.

Exciting and *entertaining* are two words used to describe the cutting-edge children's pastor. I am pretty certain that you can find exciting and entertaining children's performers that have no clue how to run a children's service. I know of young, exciting children's pastors that do not even know how to give an altar call. Charles Spurgeon once wrote, "Getting children to meet in the morning and the afternoon is a waste of their steps and yours if you do not set before them soul-saving, soul-sustaining truth."[2]

The cutting-edge children's pastor must know how to lead children in all the fun ways they enjoy. But it is imperative that she weave into this fun a depth of spirituality that will impact the children for eternity. George Barna writes, "Kids ages 2 to 7 average nearly 25 hours per week of mass media intake; the figure balloons to almost 48 hours each week among those ages 8–13. Evidence of the changing times and the new generation in place is the favorite medium of all, the Internet, according to 54% of kids under 8 and 73% of kids 8 to 12 years old."[3]

A large number of children that are served in children's church are watching around 48 hours of TV, video games, or net surfing each week. We have them in children's church for maybe and hour and a half. There is no time to waste! The cutting-edge children's pastor makes every moment count. The children's church must present a singular message preached in a variety of ways. It always ends with a time of response.

EPHESIANS 4:12 PASTORING

I am computer-dumb. I definitely am not as techno-savvy as a prospective pastor may wish. My son Tim taught me how to use PowerPoint when he was eleven years old. What I know now about computer, video, and the Internet has been learned by trial and error as much as by listening to third and fourth graders.

A friend of mine recently visited a children's church that had all the bells and whistles of technology. The team didn't minister using live costumed characters. Their characters were all shown to the children through the modern miracle of DVD projected on big screens. Songs, Scripture, and games were all projected for the children's viewing enjoyment. There is nothing wrong with showing an occasional video clip in children's church, but a cutting-edge children's pastor cannot afford to be technology-dependent. The greatest long-term impact on an individual's life in the children's church or classroom is still generated through relationship and active involvement. Kids need to interact with real people.

Ephesians 4:12 encourages us as pastors to prepare the saints for works of ministry. Jim Wideman writes, "Leaders come along side people and help them get better at what they do. They become coaches...A wise football coach wants to make each player outstanding at whatever position that player fills."[4] The cutting-edge children's pastor will share the ministry, training and encouraging others to grow in the use of their gifts.

For a number of years I led children's churches ranging from 100 to 250 children ages five through twelve. I used PowerPoint, video, overhead projectors and occasional gospel illustrations with surprise endings. I trained my workers to have back-up lessons in case of electrical failure or the occasional "audio-visual demon." I also trained my workers to involve children in positive ways to assist in teaching lessons. It is amazing how attentive a crowd of 200 children will be when several of their friends are up front holding objects for the sermon.

The cutting-edge children's pastor will use technology in creative ways. But he doesn't have to do it all himself. I have grown to trust volunteers to update the web page, develop the presentations, and send out the e-mailings. When children are in need of a physical pastor to talk and to pray with, I cannot afford to spend an entire day tweaking the next mailing on my laptop. Somebody in your church has a ministry in page tweaking. Let them soar in this ministry.

ENERGY, EXPERIENCE AND BALANCE

I am getting old. Frankly, it is a little bit harder to get up from behind the puppet stage, play soccer with the boys and girls, or stay up all night at the kids' retreat. I don't blame a pastor for wanting somebody that is full of energy. I guess younger folks are more apt to fit this point in the "cutting-edge" job description. But what the young children's pastor contributes in boundless energy is many times made up for by an older children's pastor in efficiency and impact. Being full of joy does not necessarily mean bouncing off the walls. I know very productive children's pastors, young and old, that are exciting, enthusiastic, non-hyper leaders.

I submit to the senior pastor of today that having a balanced, growing children's ministry is not "old school." The cutting-edge children's ministry of today must include ministry to the total child: physical, spiritual, mental and social.

An exciting "Nickelodeon-style" children's service *can* indicate cutting-edge leadership. The well-groomed entertaining leader may or may not be the cutting-edge children's pastor the pastor desires. Just because a leader or team can keep the kids from rebelling while someone preaches to the adults does not mean the church has the spiritual children's ministry it needs.

The cutting-edge children's pastor may or may not be young, exciting, entertaining, techno-savvy, and full of energy. She may have something deeper that breeds eternal results. That person may be someone that loves children and families, uses creative

Dick presenting a juggling lesson

methodology both old and new, and trains up an army of children and volunteers that know how to reach this dying world. That true cutting-edge children's pastor will birth a true cutting-edge children's ministry that will generate long-term growth in the church and community through relationships.

I challenge the reader to define your ministry in terms a bit deeper than *cutting edge*. The standard of what's considered cutting edge changes with time and ministerial fads. The children's pastor and his children's service must strive always to improve. In that striving they will be ever approaching the cutting edge. The rest of this book will give you practical, kid-tested children's ministry fundamentals. But this is only a beginning. If you want to be truly cutting edge, you will commit yourself to a life of learning. Become a person with a heart for people young and old, an ability to preach a solid message to children, and a lifestyle of prayer.

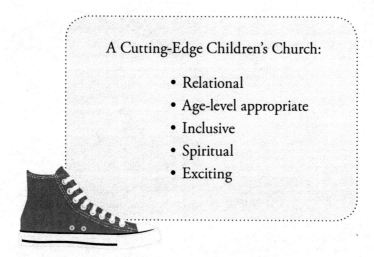

A Cutting-Edge Children's Church:

- Relational
- Age-level appropriate
- Inclusive
- Spiritual
- Exciting

from a circus to a service

There are basic rules we all live by. They begin with simple commands such as "No!" or "Don't lick the dog!" The Christian lives by the Ten Commandments, the Fruit of the Spirit, and the Law of love. Each one of us has a desire to be more like Jesus. Each one wants to do what is pleasing in God's sight.

I could not possibly continue the "cutting edge" discussion without making reference to the concept of turning your circus into a service. In the early 1980s a little-known children's ministries publication entitled *Small Steps* included a children's church article by Bob Hahn. Bob and I began our formal ministries together in children's church in Eden Prairie, Minnesota. In his article, Bob asked the question, "Is your children's church nothing more than a circus without a purpose?"[1]

Too often children participate week after week, year after year, in a three-ring attempt at church. Eventually the kids are promoted out of the children's department and are faced with the stark reality that the adults just don't have puppets and prizes each week. Such children often go through a kind of culture shock when introduced to adult worship. In many cases these children cease participating in church altogether.

The children's church should be planned with this worthy goal in mind: everything demonstrated, sung, spoken, and prayed must be done for the glory of God. All elements of a program should be working toward the day when a child graduates into sixty or seventy years of adult worship. As Bob wrote, "The Junior church must be a 'church' to our children, yet not lose its attractiveness to the fun-seeking child. In other words, we have to keep giving them Bible truths in all the interesting ways they need to hear them, but not inadvertently lie to them about their role in the Body of Christ."[2]

The children's church must be what the name implies: a training ground for the young saints of God who, because of age, are designated as children.

For this reason, the children's church worship experience should encourage children to be the church. Each child can be encouraged to participate. The church, or body of Christ, in its preadolescent form must be instructed, inspired, and instilled with militant Christlikeness.

In simpler terms, it is time to get children off the quiet seats and into the ministry. "Train a child in the way he should go, and when he is old he will not turn from it" (Proverbs 22:6). This typically dredges up dreams of well-behaved little ones happily obeying the rules, wearing mini versions of ministerial-type attire and being able to quote vast passages of Scripture. I challenge you today to think of this verse as a battle cry shouted by God himself! *Allow children to minister!*

To realize the fruit of this directive, a leader must step into daring discipleship. This calls for radical cultivation of Christlike servanthood in children who may not wear designer clothing or smell good at church potlucks. The leader must allow the children to come to Jesus in children's church. Once they arrive, the children, activated for ministry, train each other.

Picture with me the adult service. There sits an incredible pool of talent that may never rise beyond spiritual bench warming. These believers were taught in the Sunday school and children's church of yesteryear to sit quietly and listen. Week after week they were encouraged to sit, pay attention, and soak up scriptural truth. They were not allowed to hold the objects for object lessons, tell a story, run the sound system, lead a chorus, or pray for one another at altar time.

Their teachers were considered model in every way. Each class was a study in the art of discipline. Yet these students grew into lethargic adulthood. Now they sit in serene Sunday repose week after dreary week. Theses adults are doing what they were compelled to do as children. They sit quietly doing nothing for God. They have been trained in the way they should not go, and now they are old and will not depart from it.

When you try to recruit their assistance you'll hear phrases like, "I'm just not gifted with children," or "Kids aren't my thing," or "I'm just good at sitting and paying attention." Entire lives of ministry have been wasted because Sunday school teachers and children's church leaders have allowed, even compelled, children to sit still and be quiet.

There are many variations to what is called a "children's church." Some have successfully utilized the extended session. In this approach, the children

Volunteers operating a puppet in children's church

remain with their particular age groupings the entire Sunday morning. The children's church time may include a staff change and some type of song service and methodology that differs from the Sunday school. However, the extended session usually will emphasize the same theme throughout the church time as was presented during the Sunday school hour.

For the younger elementary and preschool child, this approach is fabulous. These children need the continuity of theme for the entire Sunday experience. They must be instructed through a hands-on environment that cries, "Touch and feel and discover the reality of a living God."

Let's move from the extended session to the Sunday morning circus-style children's church. The circus promotes an audience-performer atmosphere. "Hold onto your seats while the juggling puppets perform Handel's *Messiah*!" I have witnessed this praise-a-matic pandemonium hour in many forms. It occurs with disturbing frequency. The hour and a half to two hours seem to follow no theme other than that of Bible babysitting made difficult. Snacks, games, and special requests fill a time slot in which no sane adult wants to serve.

The resulting confusion, dissatisfaction, and depression among the workers cause a high burnout rate. It is no wonder that people in such a church feel that children's church is a time of babysitting. In this book we will not study these types of programs. Instead, emphasis will be placed on the "super church" concept that has become so prominent across this country. However, I will not impose sample schedules on you. Your facilities, pastor, and patience have already determined the appropriate course. Rather, I will present the ideal to strive for in making your children's church cutting edge.

The ideal is a church service where every service challenges *service*. The children we serve are saints. We encourage every saint to be a participant. They are the body of Christ and everybody should be active in the body.

So from this book, apply what will work in your setting. Underline and quote to your pastor or board those portions that may affect your future positively. Dissect and distribute the parts that will turn your children's church into a real worship experience for the children. Pray through the portions that demand a transformation of the children's church. Then make it into a training ground that provides meaningful transition into adult and family worship. In short, close down the greatest show on earth, pack away the fixings of the circus, and begin to experience the freedom of a service.

If that last statement coincides with your sense of right, then keep reading. Don't put this down until you have devoured every dogmatic delicacy within its pages. If it makes you mad, give it a chance. It may strike that chord of deeper truth that you have been searching for in your weekly struggle.

Let's look briefly at the difference between a circus and a service. A circus is noisy and confusing. So much is happening that it is hard to concentrate on any one thing. A circus is tailor-made for the attention-deficit child. The service is calm, cool, and collected. There may be noise from time to time, but all is done in decency and in order.

The circus has no central theme, while everything done in a service must preach the theme of the day. I heard Dr. Billy Graham say, "The altar call begins with the first note of the first song." Every service preaches one simple theme while aiming toward the response time.

Dick as Ernie Ushmera teaching on Acts 16:31

A circus is fun. Fun lasts for a short time and may even make a good memory. A church service is exciting. Excitement is an eternal concept. Children's church should be exciting even when it is not fun. I once had to step into children's church after spending Saturday with a man who had lost his wife and nine-year-old daughter in a car wreck. My kids knew the mom and daughter. I didn't do puppets or prizes that day. I simply talked with the children about death and eternity.

We cried together, we prayed together. Children's church was not fun that day, but it was exciting. Why? Because Jesus showed up!

The circus includes many different acts of performers. The service will have variety up front, but attempts to involve everyone. In the circus, a ringmaster ties all of these acts together. In the service, the pastor leads.

You can have a children's church. The methodology can continue to be colorful and interesting. There is still a place for your puppets and prizes; the gospel must be preached to the children in an exciting manner. But in the midst of your Sunday morning you can put the circus days behind you. You can become the leader of a valid worship service.

leadership: finding the right style

We have already mentioned some types of children's church programs. The type of program, philosophy of pastor and board, and other uncontrollable variables will determine the style of leadership you may use. At times, a person is thrust into a particular leadership style until relief comes. When it does, then the leader has opportunity to investigate and experiment with other ways to lead the children in worship. The form relief assumes is in the faithful assistance of other saints. These people may not have doctorates in children's ministries, but their zeal, teachable attitude, and faithfulness provide the help and time for reflection. I personally have used three distinct leadership styles.

Dick with Ninja Duck

When I became a children's church helper, I served on a team with other volunteers. Then, in my first years as a children's pastor, I did almost everything myself. Eventually I began utilizing and training the saints to do the work of the ministry. Now I find myself serving as a volunteer with other volunteers assisting me. (My current style closely resembles a combination of the second and third models discussed in the following pages.)

Each of the three styles presented will work in its own time and place. Take a look at them as they are described in the following pages. Examine your leadership style in light of them and then take inventory. Evaluate the effectiveness of your own style. You may want to adapt it or change it altogether. The wise leader continues to grow and learn. I have, and you can too.

HARVEY HOG SUNDAY MORNING SIDESHOW

Early in my career as a children's pastor, I produced and starred in the "Harvey Hog Sunday Morning Sideshow." Being young and unused to working with others, I found the Harvey Hog method was the easiest way to run the service.

At the time, I had not yet come to understand Ephesians 4:11–12. The Scripture plainly teaches that a teacher, pastor, or children's church leader has one major task: to prepare the saints for works of ministry. A leader who hogs the pulpit, never allowing adults or children to assist, has failed in the prime directive of Ephesians 4, verses 11 and 12.

Take a look at the characteristics of the Harvey Hog Sunday Morning Sideshow. The first requirement is that Harvey do it all. Harvey arrives at church on a typical Sunday morning with an arsenal of the latest methods. His arsenal includes puppets, prizes, an electronic keyboard (with 66 keys and over 3,000 possible sampled sounds), a puppet stage, a flannel board, an overhead projector, and a diaper bag containing anything he might need should the pastor get blessed and preach till sundown. Harvey may even have a Bible. This leader believes in the old adage, "If you want something done right, you better do it yourself, bless God!" He staggers his way toward the children's church room opening his own doors. After all, if someone else held them open they might release one too soon. The result would be catastrophic.

Harvey Hog sets up the children's church equipment behind closed doors. This is a top secret project; the eyes of others may spoil the effect of a special lesson he has planned for the children.

When the moment of truth arrives, Harvey heartily welcomes the children to church. He seats the children and calls them to order. Any stray adults that have entered the room stand at the back or exit. Harvey opens the service in prayer.

The Harvey Hog Sunday Morning Sideshow is only as well organized as the one in charge. In my case, this was a fine-tuned farce. Once in a while I even allowed my wife to take part. When I did, occasionally she knew her assignment three or four days early; at other times she knew it three or four minutes before children's church began.

If the leader in such a service is disorganized, the children will generally plan the service for him. Children are very creative when it comes to planning service or class time for the disorganized teacher. The flaw in allowing this to continue is the subject matter and methodology employed. The little darlings could be teaching something you do not want people to learn, examples being primitive methods of wallpaper removal, stacking metal folding chairs, or puppet decapitation.

All kidding aside, the Harvey Hog service will maintain a consistent quality. I have never known a Harvey Hog who was not conscientiously doing his best. At the worst, he is an untrained, misguided, boring individual. In his most advanced state, this leader can do wonders with a group of children. I have several friends who easily fit in this category. They have been "successful" children's church leaders for many years. Congregational attitudes being what they are, these leaders have done an admirable job. If you fit into this category, I encourage you to closely examine the next two and see how you might begin to involve others.

What do we know about the Harvey Hog Sunday Morning Sideshow? We know that it has these main characteristics:

- Everything done by one person (paid or not)
- No help, adult or children, allowed
- Possibly well-organized (dependent on his ability)
- Consistent quality (good, bad, or boring)

ALPHA AND OMEGA AMATEUR HOUR

A symphony of Christian ability, the Alpha and Omega Amateur Hour is a swing of the proverbial pendulum. Where Harvey has a monopoly on the ministry, Alpha and Omegas strive to produce a community effort. There is no "professional" figure pulling the strings here. There is no ambitious general pushing his way to the top.

Here you find many members with a singular purpose. This is a group of cooperative individuals who have a deep concern for the spiritual growth and well-being of the children. It was in such a group, in Eden Prairie, Minnesota, that I discovered much of the methodology that I presently use. The memories of those days are both joy-filled and scary.

A constant in every Alpha and Omega Amateur Hour is a deep commitment of the team members. The group generally consists of intelligent, caring individuals who have no great need for pastoral back-patting. They live Colossians 3:23: "Whatever you do, work at it with all your heart, as working for the Lord, not for men." In their veins run the lifeblood of faithfulness, generosity, and sincerity. These are the kind of people that support the church with their time, talents, and finances.

A typical Sunday morning will find the Alpha and Omega Amateurs hauling wheelbarrow loads of equipment into the church. They stay up most Saturday nights creating new forms of subatomic puppetry and adventures of the potato people. They creatively use the natural of every day to demonstrate the supernatural of eternity.

The Alpha and Omega crowd is prone to prayer. They recognize the need for total dependence on the Holy Spirit's guidance. There is no professional directing these saints. Theirs is a children's church guided by a strong love for the children and a unity of spirit. In most cases, these people willingly submit to whatever leadership the church provides. The Alpha and Omega team looks forward to the day when they can turn the children's church over to a genuine children's pastor. They are definitely a team committed to prayer (and people of prayer tend to be selfless).

Variety is the spice of children's church. An Alpha and Omega team provides much variety in both methodology and ability. The children will see many faces. This can be wonderful in a team that is well-organized and of one mind. On the other hand, a loosely run team, in spite of good intent, can bore, frustrate, or even confuse the children. I have painted a very positive picture of the Alpha and Omega Amateur Hour. This is a result of my own positive experience in such groups.

At the same time, I offer some cautions: should the team lack in organization, prayer, or team spirit, disaster can prevail. The Alpha and Omega Amateur Hour can very well be the circus we wish to avoid. A strong, spiritual master of ceremonies who lovingly allows all team members to express their gifts is the key to a successful team.

The church that cannot afford a children's pastor should actively recruit and train such a team as I have described. Monthly training and planning times must be provided. Let's review the basic characteristics of the Alpha and Omega Amateur Hour:

- Many members with a singular purpose
- Commitment to the Word, the church, and the children
- People of prayer
- A variety of faces and methodologies
- Depends on a competent leader to work well

FLASH AND THE FIVE REFLECTIONS

He steps to the microphone as a hush of expectancy sweeps over the children. In his hands he holds a Bible and a rubber chicken. Standing in Goliath proportion to those first graders in the front row, Flash opens the service in prayer. What follows is a finely tuned team of laypeople led through the service by this trainer of others.

Each moves with purpose; each ministers at the appointed time, as Flash ties the segments of the service to a central theme. At the conclusion, he leads in prayer and the children go out. They have encountered the living God as presented by Flash and the Five Reflections.

The most significant characteristic of this team is found in the leader. I have seen Flash in the eyes of a fifty-year-old woman as well as those of a twenty-four-year-old Bible college graduate. Flash is a person on whom the hand of God rests. He is sometimes paid for a job titled "children's pastor," a task he would gladly take on without pay. This laborer is worthy of his hire, yet would never require reimbursement for God's work.

Yes, my friend, Flash is the professional children's worker in calling, if not by title. He lives his life satisfied to be serving the most important age group in the world: children. Flash is confident in his calling. So much so that when well-meaning relatives ask, "Are you going to be a real pastor someday?" He suppresses the urge to say, "What do you mean, you ignorant buffoon? I am a real pastor." How does Flash respond? A smile, a song, a buzz handshake, and a statement something like this: "I thought I would just continue doing what Jesus would do. He would give his life for the children. Wouldn't you?" Flash finds this response to be effective.

Flash and the Five Reflections are the ultimate in Christian discipleship training. Pastor Flash recruits, trains, and inspires his children's church staff. He is an Ephesians 4:11 and 12 kind of guy. This servant of the saints knows the value of allowing the lay people to find a fulfilling place of ministry.

He knows that most of the lessons taught would be more professional, more pizzazz-filled, if he did them himself. But Flash is preparing the saints. He has discovered that a little trust in them will pay long-range dividends.

This team generally inspires an atmosphere of orderliness. It is a classic case of single-mindedness. Flash considers his team to be extensions of himself. They follow as he lovingly leads children to Christ. With numerous assistants, a variety of methodologies, and the rejection of mediocrity on his side, the service is presented. Flash moves through each Sunday morning with his team at his side demonstrating Christian unity and love. The children sense the oneness of purpose through the attitudes and actions of this team. The result is a group of children who enjoy the children's church and therefore cause little or no disruption.

In my travels, it has been a joy to step to the platform and minister in a church that has such a team. I seldom spend any time at all reminding children in such a church of my rules. They are accustomed to paying attention in a spiritually sound, understandable, quality service.

Let's look once again at the characteristics of Flash and the Five Reflections:

- Pastor with disciples (that is, volunteers)
- Ongoing discipleship training of volunteers and children
- One mind with many extensions
- Atmosphere of orderliness

I have pointed out three specific types of leaders that may run the average children's church service. The wonder of God's grace is that each of them, or variations of them, works!

However, it should be apparent to you by now that I favor a leadership style that reflects the Ephesians 4:11–12 approach. We are tasked with preparing the saints for works of ministry. Our volunteers, whether they be children or adults, are those saints. The Ephesians 4 leader, whether professional or volunteer, constantly recruits and trains others for works of ministry.

Let me encourage you to evaluate your leadership style: Is it as effective as it can be? What could be done to make it better? How could you reproduce your talent, your vision, in the largest number of people possible? Remember always to follow the leading of the greatest leader, Jesus. He mentored and coached others. Touching the children, he blessed them, setting an example for his staff and the future of the church.

a balancing act to a balanced service

In the summer of 1980 I was experiencing a ministry meltdown. Every conference I attended until then focused on methodology. Some of the biggest names in children's ministry were proposing that each children's church hour be a razzle-dazzle variety show.

One such instructor taught, "Kids are trained by the television. The average child has the attention span of a walnut. You must change activity every three to five minutes or you will lose him." "Wow!" I thought, "This must be what it is to be cutting edge."

I arrived home from that meeting and redesigned my upcoming children's church service. I interpreted the instructor's directive literally as I changed from lesson to song to chalk drawing to puppet all morning long.

I was determined to become the best vaudeville-like variety man in the business. I studied clowning, juggling, puppetry, ventriloquism, chalk drawing, music, balloon tying, and about 52 other visual methods.

My services were full of action-packed stories, up-tempo music, and bodacious surprises. Hours were spent perfecting the latest gospel magic trick, lip-syncing to the newest children's album, and practicing favorite chalk pictures. The children of my church were receiving the best in gospel entertainment.

That was the problem! The children were being entertained. They were not being ministered to, nor were they ministering.

One Sunday afternoon, following a particularly painful morning filled with children who were intent upon forcing me to redefine discipline, I announced to my wife that God had lifted his hand from our ministry to children. It was time to go and become what some people affectionately referred to as a "real pastor." Darlene simply looked at me and said, "Did you talk to Jesus about this?"

"Well, uh, not recently I haven't," was my reply.

She smiled and barked, "Then don't talk to me about it! I have to get lunch in the oven."

God is so good. He gave me an honest and caring wife who doesn't pull punches when I act stupid. With her compassionate reprimand in focus, I began to pray. I also began to evaluate exactly what I was doing each Sunday morning.

Preaching in children's church in the early '90s

My not-so-cutting-edge schedule ran something like this: Children entered the room to the most up-to-date, uptempo children's music I could blast through the sound system. I opened with prayer and a reminder of the rules. Action songs, slow songs, and a quick offering followed the opening. We then had a puppet special, a Scripture picture, an object lesson, another puppet special, an illustrated Bible story, a costumed presentation, an instrumental special, a cartoon talk, an illustrated sermon, a quick prayer, and more songs. This cluttered routine was kept in motion until the adults retrieved their children.

So what is wrong with that? Weren't the children receiving some wonderful entertainment and fine preaching? Yes, but they were not experiencing church. My service was out of balance. Children need more than well-timed puppets, phenomenal object lessons, and cliff-hanging stories. They need a service. I had failed them and they demonstrated their dissatisfaction through inappropriate behavior.

A service should contain more than the pastor's preaching for an hour. This is true even if that preaching is delivered through puppets, prizes, and a chalk drawing. After prayer and introspection, I knew that my definition of cutting edge was wrong and my circus had to be transformed into a service. Some positive steps had to be taken.

My first step was to define in as few words as possible a purpose for meeting with the children. Why did we attend service? What did I expect to accomplish during the church-time hour? What did I want the kids to know about the worship experience before being thrust into the adult worship mode?

A statement that I now deliver every week to the children came out of this time of evaluation: "We come together in this place to meet with each other and to meet with God." This is what the adults do when they attend church, the only difference being comprehension and maturity levels.

I have come to view children's church as the opportunity for an authentic worship experience, which can prepare the child for meaningful transition into adult worship. The children learn respect for church facilities, leaders, and each other in children's church. The children will be in children's church for three to six years. After this time of training, they will spend fifty or sixty years in adult worship.

The children's church service should be geared to the children's level. It should include all of the exciting methods that gain their interest, but without the loss of authenticity.

Before the child reaches the age of promotion into adult worship, I want her to know and experience Jesus Christ. She should be an active member of the body of Christ both in giving of her resources and her talent. I want to encourage in her a willingness to receive from God through the preached Word. Her developing a desire for and experience of prayer is also essential. And finally I try to cultivate in her a servant attitude by allowing her to participate in practical ministry to her peers.

If these objectives were to be met, I realized that including the basic ingredients of a church service would need to be practiced every week. After studying the typical adult worship service, I determined that four basic ingredients were needed to maintain balance. Those ingredients include:

> The four basic ingredients needed to maintain balance in a worship service:
>
> - Worship
> - Giving
> - Preaching
> - Prayer
>
> A children's church cannot be considered a cutting-edge experience without this kind of balance.

My early days of children's church were filled with exciting multi-faceted preaching but lacked the other three ingredients. I thought I really knew how to minister to kids. But there was no balance. Where there is no balance, the children's church dies. The cutting edge becomes dulled by well-meaning clutter.

Once I brought my service into balance, discipline problems dissipated, enthusiasm increased, and God began to touch all of our lives.

Adults that visit such a service never again ask, "Do you ever miss going to church?"

This balance has not been achieved at the expense of the children. The kids still enjoy the excitement of gathering with their peers. They have been awakened to the joy of meeting with Jesus. Creative methodology is still employed. The leader is not on the road to burnout.

Balance your children's church. As you digest the rest of this book, begin to apply this principle of balance and the practical ideas given for achieving it. I have employed the balance concept in five different church settings on a week-by-week basis. It has worked in each. I've used it in one-time meetings in other's children's churches. It has worked in every setting large and small. Balance is the basic ingredient in organizing a cutting-edge children's service.

worship is worth it!

I served in children's church for four years before I discovered the beginnings of worship with the kids. We had marvelous song services. No one could accuse us of dull, dreary song times. There were action choruses, dance numbers, and a much-needed slow song to calm the kids down for the rest of the service.

Psalty the singing songbook, of Kids Praise fame, once said, "You can sing songs till you're blue in the face, but if it doesn't come from the heart, it's not praise." Our blue-faced friend makes a good point. Many children's church song times do not stretch beyond a campfire singalong. Week after week, children sing songs, yet rarely worship.

Before we discovered worship, my services followed this pattern: From the time children entered the room, the air was filled with a "joyful noise." The sound system blared bouncy chords of happiness as children ricocheted off the pews. We opened the program with a shout, a quick prayer, and action songs till workers dropped. This was the way I had been taught. Somebody actually told me, "A couple of fast songs will get some of the bugs out." What nobody told me was it would also activate the adrenal gland of every moderately hyperactive child in the room. By the way, you could sing actions songs for five hours this Sunday and never put a dent in the energy level of the children.

We were not really experiencing worship.

What is worship but the personal act of ascribing worth to our loving heavenly Father? It is the orchestrated heart cry of the church in love with its Redeemer. Worship starts in the heart and spreads to the life. It is the action of a life totally sold out to Jesus, the overflowing expression of gratitude for the opportunity to live for him.

Worship is the seven-year-old girl with tear-stained cheeks praying words not memorized, but authored by the Spirit. Worship is the ten-year-old boy helping an elderly neighbor shovel snow, not for money or even thanks, but for his first love, Jesus.

In my study, I have found no passage of Scripture commanding us to teach children to worship. Oh, there are times mentioned in the Bible when children were present during worship, but I find no specific command to teach them how to worship. We are, however, compelled by numerous exhortations to teach the children God's Word.

In Matthew 21 we find Jesus preaching, teaching, and healing people in the temple area. Children spontaneously worship the revealed Christ. The religious leaders of the day wanted these embarrassing little ones to keep quiet. They should be seen and not heard.

Sam Saint telling a story

The Matthew 21 principle for children's church is this: teach the Word, experience the presence of the Christ of the Word, and children will naturally worship God. It is not hard to encourage worship when a child is healed while his friends pray. Worship is no difficulty when the Holy Spirit touches the hearts of children. The children of Matthew 21 had no charismatic cheerleader hyping them into a frenzy of happy hosannas.

Though humanity is fallen, childhood has at least a remnant of innocence. When this innocence is presented with the love of God, children raise their voices in perfect worship. Jesus quoted Psalm 8:2 when he said, "Have you never read, 'From the lips of children and infants you have ordained praise'?" He didn't finish the verse that day recorded in Matthew 21. I believe that Jesus knew the religious leaders would remember the verse continues saying, "because of your enemies, to silence the foe and the avenger."

He used Old Testament song to silence his enemies. Scripture declares the effectiveness of children's praise. God has perfected praise in the hearts and lives of boys and girls. Their honest assessment of God's worth is like no other music produced on earth.

So the task of a children's church leader becomes one of cultivating the seeds of worship that lie in the fertile soil of children's hearts. You are a gatekeeper. Each Sunday Jesus gives you the opportunity to swing wide that gate and let the praise of children out.

One method of opening the gate in any size group is the praise break. We have commercial breaks, why not praise breaks? Look through the Bible and find specific forms of praise, for example, "Be still, and know that I am God" (Psalm 46:10); "Shout unto God with the voice of triumph" (Psalm 47:1, KJV); "My mouth will declare your praise" (Psalm 51:15).

I usually hold praise breaks between songs, announcing the Scripture verse I'm using. I may say something like this: "Let us be doers of the Word today. The Bible says, 'Shout unto God with a voice of triumph!' We are all going to do what God's Word says right now. We are going to have a praise break. For the next fifteen seconds everyone in this room is going to be a doer of God's Word. We are all going to shout to God in a triumphant voice. Now, I will time you so you won't have to watch your watch. For just fifteen seconds we will shout to God. Maybe you have never done this before. That's okay. Everyone will be shouting praise to God. So when I say go, we will all shout to God for fifteen seconds."

When you're introducing the praise break concept into your children's church, it is smart to begin with short periods of time. The first time I ever held a praise break, I announced a two-minute time period. I was standing there praising God alone for about a minute and forty-nine seconds. Fifteen seconds is an ideal length for the first couple of breaks you take. After that you may grow in fifteen or thirty-second increments. Eventually you may go as long as you like.

At times we have used two verses of Scripture as praise break guidelines. A common example is the combination of "Be still, and know that I am God" (Psalm 46:10) and "lift up holy hands" (1 Timothy 2:8). The children quietly reflect on the love of Jesus while lifting their hands to heaven.

This practice for adult worship (as well as for heaven) has revolutionized my children's church. Peer pressure has been turned around. The children who once stood back and felt that loving Jesus in public was dumb or boring now willingly praise him with heart and voice. It is the acceptable practice to praise our Savior. After a slower song I might say, "Let's just be still and know that he is God." We lift up holy hands and whisper his praise.

Worship is the key to success in the continuation of your children's church service. When the kids feel his presence, circus lights fade and service life begins. When children enter into worship, discipline problems solve themselves as hearts become receptive to the living God.

What do I do for music now? When the children enter our children's church, soft, soothing praise music is playing. This could be live or taped. I prefer instrumental worship music. (Some of my buddies call it the Gruber funeral music.) I want the children to know that our meeting place is set aside for happenings of holiness. When the children walk through the door they're ready to participate in worship. Mellow worship music will allow the children to calm their spirits before God and ready themselves for a real service.

Once the children are seated and the service is opened we do begin with some action choruses and fast songs. Review what is being used in the adult or youth worship services at your church. Try to use the same songs or type of songs. Someday these kids will be in the youth and adult services. They should be prepared to make an easy adjustment into the worship offered in those settings. Remember, fast or action choruses do not work the bugs or energy out of children. That is a physical impossibility. They do bring the children together in unity of purpose.

You do not have to be a musician to lead children in worship. If your children's church lacks a regular piano or guitar player, prerecord what is needed. In my early days of children's church I used my favorite background group, "The Cassettes." Nowadays, I use CDs or DVD worship materials. The digital age makes it possible to skip or repeat songs as the Spirit leads in a service.

Dick with helpers

The children do enjoy lively music as well as slow songs. Make an effort to sing Scripture choruses as much as possible. A time or two we have inserted classic hymns in our worship time. The majestic delivery of doctrinal truths in the old hymns is needed once in a while. There are some great remakes of old hymns utilizing modern arrangements. You should have no problem obtaining any number of CDs with appropriate music for children's worship.

From the faster action-type choruses we move into some slow ones with mellow praise breaks. During these there might be time given for testimonies. We proclaim the worth of Father God through lifted hands, voices raised, and specific personal praises for his goodness to us.

Every week I tell the kids that we are in this place to meet with each other and to meet with God. This is the all-important purpose of any church service. We have fellowship with one another; this is a place of encouragement. We have fellowship with God; this is a place of refreshment.

I realize that you may not dare to step into a bold style of worship immediately. Because of your background or church tradition you may choose to move more slowly in this direction. Making small conservative changes is a wise course of action. That's all right. Just begin the action. God will faithfully bless your willingness to give worship more emphasis and freedom.

Once children have had opportunity to worship, a service follows. This is a time of serving one another. We will serve through giving, preaching, and prayer.

The ideal transition from worship to giving is a time of prayer for special needs. Some days I have the children who need prayer stand at their seats. Friends are encouraged to gather around and pray for them. Other times children with special requests come to the front of the room. I ask all others to be prayer partners. These partners stand or kneel beside or behind their needy friends and pray.

In worship we have given praise and love to God. Now, through prayer, we give support and love to each other.

Evaluate the worship in your children's church. The worship sets the tone of the service, determining its effectiveness. Without true worship, the children's church is reduced to a circus. The attitude of the leader, the music, the atmosphere, all must be built on a foundation of fervent prayer.

Hold fast to a high standard in your worship. Do all you can under the loving guidance of the Holy Spirit and then step into your worship time with confidence. Taste and see the goodness of the Lord.

Music plays a great role in leading the children into praise and a lifestyle of worship. Children love to enter the presence of God and music is a grand tool enabling this to happen. Let's look together at five great purposes for music as worship in the children's church.

Five great purposes for music as worship in the children's church:

- Inspiration
- Declaration
- Cooperation
- Presentation
- Dedication

Inspiration is the most obvious reason to incorporate music in children's worship. I get inspired hearing music at the grocery store. I find myself singing along with those easy-listening tunes. Music in church is all the more inspiring as it has a base in sound theology and Christian inspiration. Music has a profound impact on our thoughts, attitudes, and actions. A song can lift your spirit when you are depressed. It can change your heart toward one who has offended. Music can inspire you to turn your life over to Jesus.

Children seem to wear their emotions so close to the surface. Music can calm and soothe their spirits or hype them into a frenzy. Selecting the correct music to open a children's church service can do much to inspire and direct the course of the entire time you have with those children.

I have found specific songs which the children of our church look forward to singing. Most of these are slow worship choruses. When we begin such a song, kids immediately raise their hands and begin praising God. I have watched as five- through twelve-year-olds stood weeping in God's presence, inspired by a worship chorus.

Music in a children's worship service will do much to usher boys and girls into God's presence. I find that if a song inspires me, there is a good chance it will also inspire the children. For this reason, most of the music we use in children's church would more likely be associated with an adult or youth service.

Declaration is another important aspect of music in the children's worship service. We choose music that will encourage children and adults together to declare the greatness of the Lord. We tell God who and what he is in our songs. We declare the mighty wonders of our God. Children need to learn to declare God's goodness. They can proclaim the greatness of his power and grace. With no shame or embarrassment, children of my church declare through song and testimony the glory of God.

Repetition in choruses serves to burn an image of God into the hearts of boys and girls. I don't mind singing about God's holiness, power, or love over and over again with the children. By repetitive declaration of who God is and what he has done for us, we are establishing lifelong patterns of worship in our children.

My son Timothy began singing a song from church at the shopping mall one day. At first I felt like quieting him, but then joined in singing. This boy had learned to declare God's goodness in song at church. Boys and girls who pick this up in children's worship are more likely to declare God's goodness when leaving church property.

Cooperation is a great reason to include songs, both fast and slow, in children's worship. One children's church leader told me that she would lead the kids in a few rousing action choruses to get the bugs out of them. (I assume that meant she had the impression two or three rounds of "Father Abraham" would wear her kids out.) I think you know that no amount of action singing will wear the kids out before you drop over with exhaustion. The reserve of energy boys and girls have will outlast even the most fit children's church leader.

Action and fast choruses can be used to draw the kids together. Encouraging children to sing and do the actions to a song will bring unity to the body. The typical children's worship service hosts thirty or more children ages five through twelve years old. There are variations on this, but generally speaking you serve a diverse audience on Sunday morning.

Getting them to cooperate can be a chore unless you do it with music. I have found that once cooperation in singing has been achieved, it is readily maintained during the rest of the service.

Presentation of the gospel is of primary concern in our Pentecostal churches. Music is one of the best ways that I have found to present the gospel to boys and girls. Children love to learn verses and stories when presented in a musical format. When Scripture is presented musically, children seem better able to retain and restate key points of the story or verse.

It is not unusual for me to tailor my children's service around a specific song by the Donut Man, Mary Rice Hopkins, Alan Root, or other Christian children's musicians.

At one time each of our oldest hymns was nothing more than a new song presenting God's Word to the people. The theology of songs like "A Mighty Fortress," or "Blessed Assurance," is inescapable. These two and so many others have presented the gospel for many years.

When choosing music for children's worship, read through the lyrics carefully. What is the purpose for this song? Do the lyrics convey a message that is both understandable and theologically accurate? It is not enough to choose music according to the fun level. Music must be chosen with the message of the day in mind. It must be picked knowing that the possibility exists that children will repeat the song over and over again. I am very careful that the songs we sing are those that include lyrics that we want kids to repeat.

Dedication/consecration is the final of the big five. I don't think that I've ever heard Billy Graham end a crusade without the chords of "Just As I Am" playing in the background. Music seems to draw a response from the toughest street kids. I would never think of having a response time without some soft music playing. Many times, I find a song which reemphasizes the message that we have been preaching. We taught Sunday on Seeking God. During our altar time we sang "Seek Ye First."

Will you ever use a song as a bridge, or filler between service segments? It's possible. When you do, make certain the song has something to do with the theme of the day. We have no time to waste in our time with God's kids.

Let me bring a finish to this. In the church, we are always teaching children something. A rushed, disjointed, meaningless song time teaches children that music is not important. A well-planned, meaningful song service, where each song builds on the message of the last, shows thought and spirituality. Songs introducing the theme of your service show children that music is a living, vital part of the church experience. Pray as you choose music today.

giving all to Jesus

You know the story. Children's church starts and it is really going smoothly when suddenly you realize that it's offering time. Where are the buckets? Frantically you search or send someone else to search while you stall for time. Fumbling and bumbling around, your workers keep coming up empty-handed. Finally you give up on them and say, "Today we will walk past my open Bible. Let's just drop our money on its India-paper pages and be thankful that I let you out of your seat for a few moments."

Someway, somehow, offering has lost its place of honor in the children's church. If not looked upon as a time-filler or an unwanted interruption, it is reduced to competitive and questionable craziness. Like the ticket salesmen for the circus, we grab the money as fast as we can before the kids can change their minds about staying for the rest of the show.

When we relegate giving to a secondary place in the children's church, children will learn that giving is unimportant. When we treat giving as an annoying interruption, we imply that God is imposing on us. When offering time becomes nothing more than a competition for cash, children lose sight of joyous stewardship.

Please do not misunderstand me. An occasional contest can serve to increase excitement and incoming funds. But "Give and thou shall beat the girls" should not be the battle cry of the weekly offering time. God loves a cheerful giver!

I stepped into one service just as the boys were singing, "The boys beat the girls, the boys beat the girls, Hallelujah, praise the Lord. The boys beat the girls!" (Sung to the tune of "Farmer in the Dell"). I can honestly say those boys were cheerful. They were cheerfully rubbing the girls' noses in their failure to produce a winning financial report. This kind of farce fits well in a circus. But it is hardly an appropriate action or attitude for a true worship service.

When my children's church does enter the arena of competition, it is with soft steps and a godly concern. I want to see every child that makes an effort feel like a winner. Learning how to win and lose in the safe setting of the church service is not such a bad concept, but hoisting the flag of one side against the other every Sunday breeds disunity in the body. The widow's mite is still worth far more than the braggart's bucks.

Each month we set a Sunday aside for mission's education and giving. Motivational incentives are sometimes used. If a child participates with even a penny, he will be rewarded. I want every boy and girl to grow up loving missions and missionaries. Where their treasure is, their hearts will be also.

We have used all kinds of missions training ideas in our children's church. One method of educating the children about missions focuses on the passport. Each child is encouraged to bring a wallet-sized school picture. This is attached to the inside cover of a mock passport. Each Sunday for one month the child will have his passport stamped if he remembers to bring some money for the missionaries. (Again, even a penny counts.)

Keep a jar of nickels on hand in case children who visit come without any offering. At the end of the month, collect the passports and display them on a bulletin board. The prize? Satisfaction received when parents and friends recognize a job well done. Every child will feel the joy of being part of the bigger picture called missions.

In one church, I was able to arrange for live missionaries to visit our children. The pastor and I made a deal: missionaries could not speak in adult service until they had first spoken to the children. So I promised the kids that I would never introduce them to a dead missionary. Real live missionaries told wonderful stories and answered boys' and girls' questions. Each time a missionary visited our children's church, I would have the children finish his time by laying hands on him and praying for he and his family and mission assignment.

I am serious about giving. Each time the children pass the hat, bucket, or bag, they are being educated. Giving offerings is a beautiful expression of love to our wonderful Savior. Take a moment each week to give scriptural instruction on the joy of giving. My helpers are exhorted to prepare a lesson each time they are to handle offering time. A story, object lesson, or costumed presentation is a part of our giving time each week. Tithes, offerings, and missions should all be covered.

INVOLVING CHILDREN IN MINISTRY

While we are talking about giving time, it is important that we look at the concept of involving children in ministry.

My friend Verda Rubottom has written much on involving children in ministry in the children's church. She gives us these concepts to consider:

- **P**rovide good role models for kids to follow.
- **R**eserve jobs that require greater responsibility for older children.
- **A**llow children to assist in planning events.
- **I**nvolve them in small, easy-to-accomplish tasks so that they will succeed.
- **S**how appreciation for their effort.
- **E**ncouraging children to discover their gifts builds confidence in them.

When we allow a child to minister, we take a stand for God's view of everybody active in his body. Allowing children to serve in ministry...

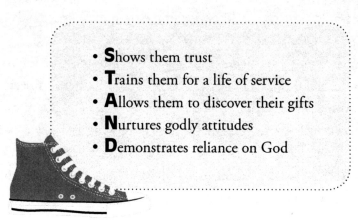

- **S**hows them trust
- **T**rains them for a life of service
- **A**llows them to discover their gifts
- **N**urtures godly attitudes
- **D**emonstrates reliance on God

TO PICK THE UNPICKABLE CHILD

I stepped out of the children's service just prior to the offering last Sunday. I reentered as the local children's pastor introduced me to the children. Seven minutes into my portion of the program, I chose two children to assist me with a lesson. Out of the almost seventy children present, I chose the same two children who had assisted with the offering. I didn't realize this until my wife, Darlene, pointed it out at lunch later that day. I had fallen into the trap of choosing the pickable children.

My family went on a vacation to Orlando, Florida. While there, we went on a studio tour during which about 200 people were shuffled from room to room. Each room held an exciting demonstration showing a behind-the-scenes look at movie making. In each separate room a group of children were chosen to assist the theme park workers in the demonstration. The same two children were chosen at random in every room. My son asked, "Why do they always pick the same kids?" That's a good question!

Let me attempt to answer that question. Some children are just pickable. Yes, I know *pickable* is not a real word, but there are some boys and girls who will be picked to help in every service they attend. I've never been able to profile these into a certain age, race, or socio-economic status. It just seems that these boys and girls have a look that draws the eyes of children's church workers. Perhaps it is their smile or the knowing gleam in their eyes. It could be their cooperative attitude. This attitude is registered in their very being as they quietly raise their hands to volunteer. Godly confidence emanates from them like a lighthouse beckoning the children's church leader to call on them.

In a children's service in which you desire to give every child a chance at ministry, what can be done about the pickable child? First, I want the reader to understand that we do not want to exclude any child from assisting, on occasion, in the service. Even the pickable child deserves to be chosen now and then. But that child should not be chosen every week nor should he or she be chosen multiple times in the same service.

Darlene noticed that the same children were often being used as helpers up front in our children's church. She started a list of children used in ministry. Each time a child was chosen to assist in a lesson, that child's name was recorded on the list. After a month of recording these names, she found that some children were used every week. Others were up front in ministry multiple times in the same service. These children

Excitement in a children's church service

were pickable kids. In a children's church that ran upwards of 200 boys and girls in attendance each week, this was unacceptable.

My wife brought this to my attention. I decided to address this issue in our next training session with children's church workers. A variety of topics were covered, one of which was the choosing of children to assist with lessons. Here are some things we taught our workers to remember in breaking the pick-the-same-child cycle:

• Do not give up on using children to help with lessons. It is important to involve children any way we can in the learning experience. Boys and girls will not only pay attention, but they will retain more of what they learn when one of their own is up front assisting.

• Pay attention! We found that while our workers did a great job up front, many times they did not pay attention to others who were involved in ministry. Consequently, a child could be chosen to help by two workers in the same service because the second worker had not even watched the first one's lesson.

• Choose the unlovely child. Look for opportunities to choose children who do not often help in any class. We found that some boys and girls had given up even raising their hands to volunteer. It had been so long since they were chosen for anything that they felt the effort of trying was lost on us. These "unpickable children" gained a new hope and excitement as they discovered our new approach.

• Ask children to raise their hands only if they have not helped already. I do this often. When it comes time to select volunteers I encourage the children already used that day to keep their hands down and give others a chance. Kids are instinctively fair-minded. Most children will cooperate when they know what you are doing.

• Keep track of those who help up front and make a concentrated effort to utilize every child in some way. Perhaps it is time to keep a list.

• Recognize that children, pickable or not, may feel a call to ministry. Encourage those with a call to use their ministry gifts. They can pray for others, work a puppet, lead in worship, tell a story, or operate sound and lights. A child being used regularly in his or her practiced ministry is not the same as an occasional helper assisting by holding an object lesson or acting out a Bible story. If you do have an active Kids' Ministry Team, ensure that children who are not official team members have opportunities to assist in your children's church.

Jesus said, "Let the little children come to me..."! He didn't say, "Let only the lovable or pickable ones come." One Sunday a visiting boy sat on the end of the second row at the center aisle of my children's church. This boy smiled and laughed at every joke. He was bubbling over with appreciation for what I was doing up front. Naturally, when the time came for me to tell a life application story, I chose him to be

Classic Sam Saint

one of my impromptu actors. He came to the front and acted like a professional. At the end of children's church, his grandmother came to meet him. They approached me at the side of the room. That is when I noticed that the boy was walking with a cane. He was totally blind! I had not even noticed his blindness. In all honesty, had I noticed, I may not have chosen him to help me up front.

God forgive me for overlooking any child because of a disability or unpickable look. Every child should have the opportunity to be in the spotlight of children's ministry. Take a chance in your children's church and pick the unpickable child.

Keep in mind that the concepts you consistently teach through actions and words today can become a blessing or curse on your church body ten years from now. The child that is trained in the joyful act of giving now may some year be the church member who supplies the finances for your new sound system in children's church.

Further, if we really believe that children are part of the body of Christ, then our giving times will provide opportunities for children to express their ministry gifts. In other words, don't let the buck stop here. Teach the children to give every resource to Jesus. Children must learn to give their time and talents as well as their money to the One who gave his life to remove their sin.

Encourage children to use talents in ministry to one another. A child may sing, play an instrument, draw a picture, or present a drama. What a fabulous place for children to experience the joy of service! Serve the Lord with gladness. You will be blessed as children receive ministry from peers and respond to God.

One Sunday a ten-year-old girl named Kari presented a song during the offering. She stood trembling at the front of the room. The background tape began to play and she opened her mouth in song. The melody was one about heaven. As her ten-year-old voice resounded, something wonderful happened. Everyone in the children's church suddenly felt as if Jesus were in the room. Some wept, others sat in silence. At the conclusion of her song, all of us prayed. Kari had, for a brief time, become the minister. God honored her preparation and my trust in her as a member of his body.

Jim and his sister Allison sang a duet during giving time. The song was one of hope that blessed everybody in the room. What an honor to allow a brother and sister to develop their talents in service of our King!

Aaron played his trumpet on a Sunday near Christmas. Sure, the tune he played isn't considered a great hymn of the church ("Up on the House Top"), but he was using his talent for Jesus. Aaron is grown now and playing his instrument in the church orchestra.

We have included children giving their talents in art, drama, reading, music, juggling, doll collecting, and model building. The intent behind this is to find out what a child can do and allow him to do it for the glory of God. If a boy loves to fly model rockets, then have him bring one to class. As he shows it, teach about rising above the sin of this world.

Allow the children's church to become the church of the children! Create a balance that includes giving. Children will realize that you are indeed a good shepherd. Your willingness to prepare the young saints for works of ministry will payoff in adults who feel a call to active service for the King. Someday a Sunday school teacher or missionary will stand and testify that she began ministering as a child in your children's church. That is where she discovered the wonderful feeling of being used by God to touch others. Giving of herself in ministry became a habit that the turmoil of the teenage years couldn't break.

In the meantime, your youth pastor will be blessed as you promote a ready force of ministers into his department each year. Parents will be amazed as their children relate incidents week after week of God's power demonstrated in and through the ministry of their peers. The greatest joy I have experienced in children's ministries has been witnessing God's hand on the ministry of a particular child, to watch children grow in concern for the lost, and to see a tangible expression of that concern.

Each children's church leader must ask at one time or another, "Am I raising an army of pew potatoes?" Children who are told week after week to sit down and be quiet will eventually do just that. Then as adults they will quietly sit and do nothing for God, for this is what they learned in children's church. Begin this week to train up the children in the way they really should go. Teach them to joyfully assist with songs, tell a story, or help their neighbor. Train them in godly attitudes of service to others.

Who knows? Five years from now you may have a full force of willing, well-trained helpers who first caught the vision for ministry in your own children's church. Consider the giving time as recruitment for the future workers of the children's church. Allow children, the church of today, to give of their finances, their talents, their lives. Let them come to Jesus in complete joy and service. Teach them how to be willing vessels of honor for God.

Your faithfulness in this aspect of children's church creates a wonderful readiness in boys' and girls' hearts. They have worshiped Jesus in song, testimony, group prayer, giving of tithes and offerings, and ministry to one another. They are now ready to receive from God's Word in your preaching time.

get the message, then the puppet

If you are anything like me, preaching is one of your favorite activities. It rates right up there with snorkeling off Maui, playing expensive keyboards, or eating chocolate peanut butter ice cream.

Preaching is about the most natural thing a Christian can do, next to breathing. Christ commanded every believer to "Go ye into all the world and preach the gospel to every creature" (Mark 16:15 KJV).

These kids are engaged in the service

What a grand privilege it is to share the good news of Jesus with others! This opportunity is enhanced when you realize that God has allowed you to preach to his most precious souls: children. You are preaching in the children's church to those who best represent Christ in this world. If you give a cool cup of water to one of these little ones, you have given it to Jesus.

Perhaps you do not feel much like a big-time preacher. The words seemed to come so easily to the likes of Paul, Apollos, Luther, or Wesley. But remind yourself that God has chosen the foolish things of man to confound the wise. Ordinary people who received an extraordinary anointing of the Holy Spirit preached the great revivals of history.

God is looking for a willing servant. You have been chosen to preach a life-giving message. Perhaps you have felt as if you were an accident waiting to happen. You were recruited, stuck in a children's church room, and left on your own. Do not fear! God loves the children of your church so much that he appointed you as part of their special ministry team. You are perfect for the job. A great harvest of souls is waiting for your faithfulness.

The preaching time is that portion of the service when a message from God is transmitted to the child. But where do you get such a message?

I strongly believe that the whole message cannot be found in a curriculum of any kind. Do not misunderstand. There are many fine curriculums on the market today. Each year it seems yet another creative children's pastor floods the market with her version of the perfect children's service curriculum.

When choosing a curriculum, begin to think of its intended use. Curriculum is a recipe card. You are the Master's chef. God has allowed you the freedom to add to, or take away from, the content of curriculum and no curses will come upon you. Gather the ingredients that will best convey the theme to your children and make it palatable to them.

Would you invite your friends over for Sunday dinner and feed them recipe cards? Of course not! Even as they would expect a prepared meal, so would the children you serve. A pastor would not last long at any church if he read or recited Charles Spurgeon sermons every week. People expect the pastor to deliver a fresh word from the Lord. Children expect and need a fresh message from God in your preaching time each week.

If you are in the process of choosing a curriculum, let me give this simple bit of advice: look first to your own denomination. If your denomination publishes a children's church curriculum, then that is the best source for you. My reasoning is simple. A quality curriculum published by your denomination will be the only curriculum that teaches doctrinal specifics the way you believe it. Look to your denominational publishing house before spending big bucks on independent curriculums. Chances are you will receive just as much or more content than that in some of the fancy full-color notebooks available on today's market.

The curriculum becomes a base for a message from God. You may consult many other curricular sources in the preparation of that message. But please do not read word-for-word what was written by some other hand for a wide-spread audience of believers.

I look to the curriculum for a basic theme. Then I pray for God's anointing. I pray that God will give me a message as I study that theme in the curriculum and in his Word, the Bible.

Each day you should set aside time to pray and meditate upon that which you will teach or preach next week. A little a day keeps the burnout away. The Saturday night special may work for you once in a while, but soon the children will know that you are not prepared.

Ernie and his teddy bear

Discipline will break down and the circus will begin.

In the preaching portion of children's church there are three things I always want to have: Scripture verse, Bible story, and illustrated sermon. I may or may not add puppets, object lessons, chalk talks, costumed characters, life application stories, or a host of other methods. Keep in mind that the message is more important than the method.

I first look to God for the message; then I look to what methods will best speak to the children. Remember to always use language and concepts that the youngest child present will understand. Do not speak down to the children; talk with them. Be normal. There is nothing worse in a child's eyes than an adult that suddenly takes on a phony personality when preaching to kids. Be yourself and use language that will be understood.

There have been Sundays when I have simply addressed the children with an open Bible. Other times I go nuts with zany methods that expand the message before their eyes.

Try as often as possible to use all of the senses in preaching. One leader I know baked fresh bread on a Sunday morning. That day, the children smelled the message. They saw it, touched it, tasted it, and finally heard it as the leader preached about Jesus, the Bread of Life. You can be sure the kids will remember that message. Every time one of them enters a bakery he will think, *Jesus is the Bread of Life.*

Church is always exciting when Jesus arrives. There may come times when you must deal with tough subjects that are not fun or that do not lend themselves to fun methods. Do not shy away from them. Trust Jesus and preach with confidence.

Do all you can to involve the children while preaching your message. There are extroverted kids that will volunteer to act out every Bible story. Give them the opportunity. But do not fail to recognize the quiet children as well. A quiet or shy child can hand out papers, hold the object of an object lesson, or keep score in a quizzing contest. Involvement rates right up there with repetition as a key factor in learning retention. A child who participates in a lesson will be more apt to remember and apply that lesson throughout the week. Children can teach and preach to other children. As part of the body of Christ, every boy and girl has some ministry waiting to be discovered. Look for ways to allow children to serve children during the preaching time. I have found that object lessons are good, short, entry-level lessons for interested ministry hopefuls.

What methods are acceptable? I do not know your church as you do. Look to the leadership of your local body for direction. In one congregation the use of clowning and magic is no big deal, while in another it can be offensive. If I discover a method offends someone, I discuss it with that person, or cease using the method.

I personally have tried many different media and methods, including role-play, drama, costumed characters, clowning, mime, drawing, chalk talks, puppetry, ventriloquism, juggling, storytelling, slides, overhead projector, audio and video tapes, shadow puppetry, music, fire, magic, object lessons, discussion, games, Scripture pictures, breakfast cereal, puzzles, chalkboard, and flannel-graph.

I get ideas at conventions, toy stores, grocery stores, television, and from my own children. God is the most creative force of the universe. His Spirit dwells in the life of every believer. Draw upon this heavenly reserve and present your message in a creative new way this week.

Once a quarter we have game show Sunday. The theme will generally revolve around the idea of choices in life. Every game that is used will incorporate the theme in some memorable way.

We also like to invite a missionary on occasion to preach the entire service. Kids need to see that missionaries are real people. They must be exposed personally to these men and women of God. It is through such encounters that God calls children to full-time Christian service.

I was told by a man once that he was "ready to preach, pray, sing, die, or testify at a moment's notice." Does that ring a bell? In the children's church you will have times that call upon your deepest reserves. The puppet may fall out of the stage, your object lesson may not work, or the kids may be bored with your presentation. Be ready in your preaching to change direction with the flow of the Spirit or the attention span of the children.

A well-prepared, prayer-soaked message will withstand broken sound equipment, undisciplined bus kids, or parental interruptions. Check your message this week. Have the children of your church been drinking from the well or has it been an occasional sip from a rusty bucket? Pray for God's anointing and his best each time you step into the preaching portion of your children's church. The preached Word of God will change lives, bring healing, and free boys and girls who are in the bondage of this world. Let all that you do lead to a time of response.

THE SERMON

When preparing a children's sermon, I first meditate on the theme and memory verse of the day. I pray and ask God what he wants to say to the boys and girls on a given Sunday. I believe that God has a message each week that can radically change the lives of the children. Here are some things I keep in mind as I prepare my preaching time in children's church:

- The message is more important than the method.
- Keep It Simple, Saint.
- Make sure that what you say and do is scriptural and doctrinally sound.
- Illustrate the message using pictures, objects, and stories.
- Prepare your material so that it will be easily understood by the youngest child in the room.
- Stick with one major theme.
- Try not to be confusing.
- Be genuine in all you say.
- Preaching should be loving, not scary.
- No baby talk.
- Talk to them, not at them.

In April 2001 Adam Schmidgall, children's pastor in Ogden, Utah, taught a class on preaching to children at a conference I attended. The following notes are my interpretation of Adam's fabulous teaching. Remember to be personal with the kids. Let them get to know you and you will be more effective when preaching to them. This connection is more important than good homiletics.

PREPARING TO PREPARE THE SERMON

- Be a person who knows Jesus.
    - ✓ Know him personally.
    - ✓ Know how he taught. How did he do everything?
    - ✓ Know what this means for us. Let him transform you.
- Be a person of prayer.
- Be a person who understands kids.
    - ✓ Understand your audience.
    - ✓ Use your own memories. What was it like when I was a kid?
    - ✓ Use what you know.
    - ✓ Use what you can learn. The children's pastor is always growing in Christ.
- Be a person kids want to hear.
    - ✓ The Jesus factor—his love attracts kids.
    - ✓ The human factor—be real with kids.
- Be a person who knows what you are getting yourself into.
    - ✓ Know your audience.
    - ✓ Know your setting.
    - ✓ Know your calendar.

PREPARE THE SERMON

Twelve steps:

1. Don't forget to pray.
2. Choose a biblical direction.
3. Find supporting texts.
4. Determine your subject.
5. Find the Application Point—The one theme you will nail to the wall—something to think about, something to do, something to realize, a phrase they repeat.
6. Form an outline—2 to 4 points, no more—Use who, what, when, where, why, and how questions. Use deduction, be creative.
7. Find illustrations—Determine what you will need, know your text. Use what you know, techniques, stories, or what you've seen. Determine the methodology: visuals, hands on, includes involvement, quotes and stories, use the senses.
8. Gather and arrange props, visuals.
9. Practice and think through your sermon.
10. PRAY!
11. Do what works best for you.
12. Don't be afraid to ask for help.

PREACH THE SERMON

- Be prepared.
- Get the kids involved.
- Engage their minds.
- Use their names.
- Ask questions.
- Pull them in.
- Have them repeat points.
- Use motions.
- Use sound effects.
- Use visuals.
- Think ahead, expect the unexpected.

beyond a little talk with Jesus

A well-balanced children's church service includes worship, giving, preaching, and finally, prayer. Children are wonderful when it comes to prayer. They pray for dogs and cats and television personalities and stuffed ducks. You tell a child that God wants us to pray, and he will do it. But where does a child learn how to pray?

In the home, prayer or lack of it is taught at the dinner table and bedside. It is experienced in the knocks and victories of everyday living. A wise parent does not relegate prayer to a twice-a-day-only-when-we-have-to kind of activity. Prayer can and should be woven into every part of a child's life.

This is a day of broken and blended families. Prayer does not always receive the emphasis it deserves in the home. It is important to give prayer a place of prominence in the children's church. You have opened the service with prayer, prayed for special needs, and prayed over the offering. Before the children even arrived in the room, you prayed for a message from God and an anointing on the delivery of that message. You pray with your staff and with children who will minister in this week's service.

TEACH US TO PRAY

When the disciples approached Jesus concerning prayer, he did not turn away. They said, "Lord, teach us to pray." Jesus then set a pattern with what we call the Lord's Prayer.

Like the disciples of old, children desire a pattern. I believe children are looking to you and me for instruction in this area. Again they are crying, "Teach us to pray!" Paul exhorted the church to "pray without ceasing." Tell that to a seven-year-old and he will reply, "How?"

Your example, attitude, and love of prayer will become important instructional tools. Only the depth of your love, and continuing relationship with Jesus limits frequency of prayer. Children learn by your life that prayer is not just a tool of acquisition. It is a time of acquaintance with your first love, Jesus. Prayer must appear important to you if it is to gain importance in the lives of the children you serve. We know that fabulous things can and do happen when people pray in faith believing.

Once in our children's church in Minnesota, a need was brought to our attention. A little girl told me in a worried voice about the son of a man who worked with her dad. The boy was hurt in a sledding accident. She could not tell us his name but she knew that he was in critical condition. I stood a child in the middle of the room, the children laid hands on him, and prayed for the nameless boy. After prayer time our service continued. On Tuesday morning, I found the boy and his mother at the hospital. She told me that on Saturday evening doctors had instructed her and her husband to begin funeral arrangements. The boy had multiple internal injuries, some of which had destroyed vital organs. She reported that on Sunday morning, at exactly the time we had prayed, her son had been healed. The boy pulled out the plugs and asked his mother for something to eat. I can't explain the healing power of Jesus. I only know that he inspired the writer to say, "Cast your cares on him for he cares for you." Jesus does care for every boy and girl in every family.

He is a personal, loving Savior who desires the best for his children. When Jesus physically walked this earth, he took children in his arms and touched and blessed them. I believe he is still touching and blessing the lives of boys and girls today. So allow for that opportunity.

A TIME FOR RESPONSE

Make everything you pray and say and demonstrate in the children's church service point to a time of decision. Your entire service should culminate in a designated time of response. If you wish, call it an altar call. This time of prayer is singularly important and should not be forgotten or rushed. As previously mentioned, Dr. Billy Graham says, "The altar call begins with the first note of the first song."

The following scenario has happened in almost every children's church. There are variations, but the pattern is constant. You encourage the children to bow their heads in prayer. In your most serious tone, you invite response to the day's message. Some children raise their hands or come forward for prayer. Soft music is playing and the presence of God is real.

Suddenly the back door bursts open and Mrs. Fluster dashes into the room. Bless God, church was good but now it's over. Pastor began his altar service and Mrs. Fluster needs to grab little Mary and run for the car: "Dinner is going to burn and it's Super Bowl Sunday. Papa Fluster is out revving up the Chevy, so grab your Bible and run!" Her hurry is evident as she trips over chairs looking for little Mary. Her wonderful daughter is praying at the far side of the altar. Mother grabs Mary and drags her from the room. Your prayer time is destroyed. Any work God had begun is now terminated.

Scenario two is the quick prayer and run. In the middle of your illustrated sermon, an usher steps through the back door, signaling that church is out. Parents begin peeking their heads in and you know you had better end the service. You close in a quick prayer and the children leave. Again your children's church has ended in frustration.

I have discovered a couple of little tricks for doing away with these kinds of frustrations. You can close and lock your back doors. Place a large sign in bold print on the door saying something like, "Work of God in progress. Do not interrupt the work of the Holy Spirit. Please wait outside until children are dismissed." One children's church leader painted a sign that read, "Do not enter. Negatives being exposed to the Light."

Of course you can always place a former pro-wrestler at the door to help parents wait. Chances are, this kind of approach will be met with some disbelief or even animosity from the parents. We do, from time to time, place a polite assistant at the door to calmly keep the parents from entering during prayer.

However, the early altar call seems to be the easiest solution to disrupted prayer. Time has been set aside to allow children plenty of opportunity for prayer. Here is how to plan for adequate prayer time.

Son Tim posing as a Christmas tree

Check the average estimated time of departure. At our church, the morning adult service is usually over by 12:15. That is our estimated time of departure. Back up from this time, fifteen to twenty minutes. This is your designated altar service time. In my case, the prayer time is set at 11:55 each week. This gives us plenty of time to pray without adult interruptions. I have had weeks when the children took all of that time and more. Then again, there are times when they pray for two or three minutes and then stare at me. When this happens we play Bible quiz games or present a reinforcing object lesson.

Each Sunday one of my helpers is assigned the duty of having a lesson ready for post-prayer emergency. Then, if allotted prayer time is not used up, we are not caught flat-footed. Bible quiz games can always reinforce what we have learned that day.

Now you ask the question, "What do you do in the prayer (altar) time?" As with the rest of the service, I want the children to be active participants in prayer. Never allow prayer to become a boring exercise. Use different methodology from week to week.

While the prayer time is underway I always play mellow praise music in the background. I have listed, with explanation, several methods we employ in order to keep prayer time interesting.

ALTAR CALL

This is the Billy Graham-type approach. The theme for the day is emphasized and children are encouraged to respond individually. A child wishing to respond raises his hand and is asked to stand and walk to the front of the room. Upon arrival at the altar a helper meets and prays with him. From time to time, a prayer is recited and repeated by those responding. At the conclusion of any prayer time, children are escorted back to their seats.

ALTAR SERVICE

In this prayer time, all children are asked to stand. We gather them all about the altar at the front of the room and together we pray and sing worship songs. These have been some of the most precious prayer times I have experienced.

PRAYER AT THE CHAIR

The children are asked to kneel at their seats and pray. Those with special needs or wanting a prayer partner are told to raise a hand. My workers and I circulate around the room praying for special needs. When a child is done praying he can quietly sit in his chair or sing along with whatever praise music is playing.

SMALL GROUPS

From the front of the room I divide the boys and girls into groups of four or five. This is not a matter of their choice: I assign each child to a group, with whom he will pray. I then direct the groups to various corners of the room, where they are led in prayer by one of my helpers.

PRAYER PARTNERS

Divide the kids into groups of two. The two exchange names and phone numbers and pray for each other during your altar time. Then they call each other on the phone throughout the week and share in prayer.

CIRCLE PRAYING

If your group is small enough or you have a large room, stand in a circle holding hands. Pray around the circle, each child making his or her requests known out loud. A child not wanting to speak out loud may simply say, "unspoken," or squeeze the hand of the next child, signaling him to pray. The leader can close in prayer, mentioning both the spoken and unspoken needs.

A FEW THOUGHTS ON ALTAR CALLS AND CHILDREN

Jesus said, "Let the children come to me..." He did not say, "drag, coerce, push, force, threaten, or browbeat them to come to me." Over the years, altar calls for and with children have included many different styles, uses, and sad to say, abuses. Some leaders have used inappropriate pressure to compel children to respond at the altar. I have watched and listened as pastors or evangelists have told scary stories to coerce children to come to the altar.

On the other hand, I have witnessed loving invitations given to children. I have watched boys and girls using ministry gifts as they pray with others. I have participated in many prayer services where children have been saved, healed, and delivered at altars.

The altar call or alter service should be a positive experience for children. Workers must be sensitive to God's leading and encourage children to pray one for another. Physical contact should be limited to a hand on the shoulder, head, or back. When appropriate, a hug may be given to a child. Cry with the children. Laugh with them. Above all, enjoy the presence of God with them at the altar.

We encourage boys to pray with boys and girls with girls. In the mid to upper elementary ages, more distraction is evident when children pray for those of the opposite sex. Nothing should be allowed to distract children from meeting with God.

The leader giving the altar call must speak with confident authority. God has placed him or her in this service for such a time as this. Many times the altar call is referred to as the "invitation." Think of it as an invitation and you will stay away from improper attitudes, actions, or words. A loving, Christ-like calling out of those wanting to respond will reap great results.

I often encourage every child to spend a little time with Jesus. Children are directed to find a place to pray at their chairs or at the altar area. What a blessing to see children turning and kneeling to pray. What a thrill I've experienced in children's church when joyfully praying with boys and girls at the altar.

I've listed some things below to do and say when giving an altar call or ministering around the altar. I trust that these will help you to better sharpen this ministry skill.

THINGS TO DO:

- The theme is repeated throughout the service.
- Pray about the established theme.
- Speak with God's authority.
- Use kid-friendly language/concepts.
- Keep It Simple, Saint.
- Repeat instructions as needed.
- Relax, let God do the work.
- Pray for this part of the service.
- Give a variety of options such as pray at chair, altar, alone, with friends, stand, sit, kneel.
- Encourage those not praying to worship and be respectful.
- Compliment those not praying for showing respect to God and their praying friends.
- Play slow worship music that is familiar to the children.
- Direct children to pray for other children or adult helpers.
- Let them pray as long as needed.
- Be positive in your approach. For example: "I know some of you are ready to pray today…"
- When most are done praying, close in prayer. You may want to sing a song with the children as they go back to their seats.

THINGS TO SAY:

- Some of you want to respond.
- Put your faith and trust in Jesus.
- Ask Jesus to come into you life.
- Trust Jesus to be your best friend.

- Ask God to forgive the wrong things you've done.
- We call the wrong things we do, "sin."
- Only Jesus can clean the sin out of our lives.
- Jesus wants to save us from the destruction that sin causes.
- You may all find a place to pray right now.
- You can pray at this altar or turn and pray at your chair.
- Pray/repeat after me.
- If you want special prayer, raise your hand. A worker will come and pray with you.
- Prayer time is time to meet with God. That's why we are not talking or playing with friends right now.
- I want to thank you for showing respect to God and your friends by sitting quietly or worshipping Jesus when you are done praying.

THINGS NOT TO DO OR SAY:

- Ask Jesus into your heart.
- Just let go.
- Just hang on.
- Sin is black.
- If you've done this before, do not come down.
- Give your heart to Jesus.
- Come let the blood of Jesus wash you.
- Pray now or go to hell.

Often at the conclusion of our prayer time, I will encourage children to tell an adult worker or friend what God has done for them. This seals the spiritual experience with a conscious physical act.

Pray for creativity in your prayer service. Give adequate time for this most important portion in the balance of your children's church. An imbalance in this area will send children home with no practical application to the message. Please do not plan a wonderful lesson and leave them wondering how it applies to their lives.

Time spent in prayer is always worthwhile and will many times lead to life-altering decisions. God can do much to change even the most unruly child during a serious moment of prayer.

As one friend of mine said, "Why spend all that time in preparing and presenting a message and close with no time of response?" Give children the privilege of being touched by God. Give them a weekly time of prayer and commitment of themselves to him. Promotion day will come and the kids will begin to attend the adult service. Your pastor will be blessed to see an honest, open response in these who have learned that prayer is an important part of every service.

At the conclusion of the response prayer time, I typically give the kids two or three ideas for immediate application of the lesson. This may take the form of helping mom without complaining or showing mercy to a younger brother. After this, we close our service with prayer.

allowing parents to participate

You have just experienced a fantastic service. At the conclusion, parents are stopping by to take their children home. Suddenly some well-meaning mom steps from the crowd and, wringing your hand, says, "Thank you so much for watching our kids. I don't know what we would do on Sunday mornings without you."

She thinks you are babysitting. Of all the nerve! What is the matter with her?

The matter is that you have never trained this woman or the other parents. She doesn't know you are having church. How will parents ever know you are having a service if you do not allow them to visit once in a while?

Remember, the biblical pattern has always been that parents take the lead in teaching spiritual concepts to their children. Scripture is packed with exhortations to Mom and Dad concerning this mandate. Parents are compelled to teach their children about God.

Parents are not only the prime Christian educators of their children, but they are fully equipped by God for this task. So what better workforce is there in the church to teach and reach the children than parents?

"Parents, instruct your children in the Word of God. Do this while you are walking down the road, watching television, out for pizza, sitting around the dinner table, shooting hoops, or preparing for bed.

"Do this so that they will know and love Jesus every day. Do this so that their Christianity will have meaning every hour. Do this so that they will grow up and teach their children of the love of Jesus" (Deuteronomy 6:7–9, Gruber paraphrase).

Parents must take an active part in the child's church experience. This is not only biblical, but it gives you extra helpers on Sunday morning.

The Grubers in Texas, 1985

Now you are going to ask, "How can I get parents out of the adult service and into the real world?" Adults love to worship God without the interference of children. Kids love to worship God without the interference of parents. So how are you going to merge the two?

The task is not easy. You must commit yourself to a campaign of education that will encompass every church publication. This noble crusade will impose upon your personal time, in phone calls and visitation. It will eat away at your office hours and tax your administrative competence.

Do all you can to inform the parents. Send home a note each month notifying them of the theme and reinforcing Scripture that will be used in your children's church. You may want to include ideas for carrying the theme into family life and devotions.

Use every church mailer and bulletin to carry testimonies of the goodness of God in your children's church. The printed word will get through to some of the parents.

Every time you see the pastor, give him a short praise report regarding your service. Many times he hears from you only when your ministry has a financial need. Condition him to believe that there is something spiritual happening in your children's church. (Be honest, of course.)

Set a goal of visiting each child's home. This is great for building rapport with the child as well as with the parent. In your visit share the beauty of the children in worship, the wonder of their ministry in the giving time, the joy of preaching to them, and the power of your altar times. However, do not recruit in your visit to the home. Let the home be a sanctuary from high-pressure sales. Once you get to know the parent it is much easier to ask for help when needs arise.

We have "Meet the Saint" scheduled as a regular feature in our children's church. This is a time when the children can meet a parent or other church member. The saint is asked to visit the service on a specified Sunday. He will not have to prepare a lesson or preach to the children.

The only requirements for this are (1) that the person is a Christian, (2) that he be living for Jesus, (3) that he arrive before children's church begins, and (4) that he stay until "Meet the Saint" time.

You guessed it! "Meet the Saint" time is usually held at the end of the service. I want that saint to experience the entire children's church service. I want him to see that we are not babysitting; we are not having a circus.

The "Meet the Saint" guest-initiate is invited to come to the front of the room. The children's church leader interviews him. I want the kids to know that a housewife or insurance agent or carpenter or trash collector can live for Jesus. Interview the person and leave a short time for questions from the kids. At the end of this time, thank the saint and encourage the kids to greet and talk to him whenever they see him in church or in the community.

We have had a variety of people in for "Meet the Saint." The most memorable among them include a soldier and a church board member.

The soldier was a marine sergeant. He came in full battle fatigues and spoke of being both a Christian and a soldier. It was a fabulous testimony. Many of our boys found a real-life GI Joe for a hero.

The board member came and shared his occupation. He then told about the duties of a deacon and spent time praying for every child. It was a very touching time in our service as he laid hands on children and prayed. (When your board members experience the service, you no longer have trouble with requests for equipment.)

"Meet the Parent" is another program that works in bringing parents into the children's church. With this concept, children are encouraged to sign up for a Sunday where all of the children's church gets to meet the parent. On the appointed day, a child brings his or her parent(s) to children's church. The adult sits with his child until meet the parent time. The entire family is then invited to the front of the room where you conduct a short interview, pray for this family, and take a couple of instant-developing pictures of

Dick with granddaughter Isabella

them. One picture is placed in a frame and given to the family as a souvenir. The other is placed in a photo album at the back of the room where children can page through, seeing their family as well as others anytime they enter the room.

Another way to get parents through the door is to set up a schedule requiring their attendance. Parents can sign up or submit to the draft. Do not put them up front as a minister but rather in the seats with the kids as a participant. Allow them to join the congregation in worship, giving, preaching, and prayer.

Parents should participate as much as possible in every outing, field trip, or party you throw for the children. Moms and dads need this kind of ministry experience. A wise administrator will seek a one to four parent-child ratio at such events. Parental involvement or lack of it can make or break these types of events.

You will want to include parents in any and every service and activity you can. This comes by prayer, fasting, phone calls, and personal notes. It can be a long and difficult process, but the parents will begin to catch your vision. Without a vision, the children's church will perish.

Begin right now to think of the parents as friends. Build friendships with them and discover a truth I learned long ago: it is hard to quit a friend. Pray for wisdom in this. Enjoy the beauty of it as God faithfully assists you in strengthening families through the children's church.

One last note: be sensitive to the single parents. Many of the children you minister to are from single parent or blended family homes. (Make special allowance in your attendance contests for the child who is there only twice a month. He has no control over the parent who fails to bring him to children's church.)

When you hold special parent-child events, arrange for adopt-a-parent as the need arises. Take time to listen to, comfort, and provide spiritual and physical assistance for these families.

I am from a family that was broken by divorce. It was not an easy situation, but God in his rich mercy worked through a few faithful saints to supply help when needed.

Be open to what God would have you do with the parents of your church. If you stay there long enough, you will witness today's children becoming tomorrow's parents. The parents of today will be grandpas and grandmas. You will be blessed as you minister to the next generation side by side with these concerned Christian models.

Share your vision; involve the parents. I know you are not a babysitter and you know you are not a babysitter, but you want parents to know this too.

smorgasbord

This chapter is devoted to all of the little things I wanted to say to you. Most of the items fall into the category of practical advice. I feel they will be of interest and help to you. So look upon this as a kind of smorgasbord of children's church wisdom.

CREATIVITY

I have been approached many times by teachers and leaders of children who have said, "I am not a creative person. I can't tie balloons or sing or draw chalk pictures." Perhaps you sit there thinking similar thoughts right now.

Sam Saint and his keytar

Forget it! You are creative. You are created in the image of God! His Holy Spirit dwells in the heart of every believer. The creative force of the universe, Jesus Christ, has taken up residence in your life. You are creative.

Do not mistake methodology for creativity. Any person can attend seminars and schools to learn visual methods. The average uncoordinated person can learn how to juggle, use puppets, and even trace a picture onto a sheet of butcher's paper. This does not, however, involve the creativity level of that individual.

One dictionary says *create* means "to produce through imaginative skill." It is the act of bringing into existence something new. This creativity is part of your ministry arsenal. Expertise in several methods will increase this arsenal. You will have greater ease in capturing the attention of the kids as you use your God-given creativity.

Perhaps your imagination has been idling for some time. Give it a tune-up and begin to create. Use creativity in your everyday life. Step beyond the mediocre norms in your approach to problem solving and simple survival. Cultivate this God-infused creativity.

Bible verse Rebus puzzle

Open your eyes and see the excitement of living in this colorful world. Study God's creativity through the good earth around you. It is amazing to discover what God has created. Look in the mirror. Smile a while and give your face a rest.

When I am not feeling very creative, I do one of two things. First, I spend time observing my children at play. Children have not yet unlearned creativity. Their play is, without reservation or adult intervention, filled with imagination. Simple blocks become airplanes or animals. Anything with wheels can drive through large cities, cultivate fields of crops, or explore jungle paths.

If watching my children doesn't inspire me, I view an hour or two of public television, go to a toy store, or involve myself in home improvement projects. Yes, pounding nails helps me generate ideas for children's church.

Above all, be yourself. If God had wanted Dick Gruber to teach in your children's service each week, he wouldn't have placed *you* there. You are God's perfect choice for those kids at this time. Be creative in your presentation and the children will gladly respond to the message.

ENVIRONMENT

Step into your children's church room. Place a paper sack over your head and listen. Listen to the sounds of the room. What noises are entering from the great beyond?

Now take the sack off and kneel down. From a child's vantage point, look around and observe the room. Is it colorful? Is it boring?

While on your knees you begin to see the room as the children do. Viewing it from the child's eye level you may notice that chalkboards are too high on the wall or visuals are not easily seen from the back row. Take time to pray while still on your knees. Pray that God will help you to make this room more visually appealing.

Move to a chair. Is it the right size for little boys and girls? Scrunch down in the chair. Now your eyes are at the level of the child who sits there. Can he see your face, puppets, other visuals? Will his view cause him to squirm and move and disrupt your worship?

Basically I am telling you to think like a child. View your facility through the eyes of a child. Children do not want to enter a room made for giants. They want to sit in a chair the right size and still be able to see the lesson being presented.

Smell your room. Does it need a good airing out? Buy some air freshener (not the kind that smells like a hospital). We once had a room in the basement of the church. This room had off-green walls, black tile floor, and smelled of must and bathrooms. We painted, covered the floor with carpet, took care of the humidity problem, and installed ventilation fans in the bathrooms. What a difference. Children could actually learn in the new environment!

If your room is cluttered and musty and drab, you cannot hope to hold the child's attention. Environment can cause discipline frustrations for even the best of teachers. Take care of your classroom and it will become a help instead of a hindrance to your ministry.

By the way, clean up after yourselves. If the kids trash the place during game show Sunday, bless them with the thrill of cleaning it up. Teach them to be good stewards of church properties in this way.

DISCIPLINE

I believe in discipline. A well-ordered children's church service is healthy for the spiritual formation of children. But there is a difference between discipline and punishment.

Punishment is a temporary answer to an eternal problem. Discipline holds an eternal answer. Punishment focuses on getting even. Discipline helps a child build a positive self-image and grow in self-control.

Punishment says, "If you do that one more time, I am going to send you to the adult service to sit by your parents." You have just taught the child that it is punishment to sit in church by her parents, that it is punishment to listen to the pastor preach. So when she is promoted out of your department and the doors to the children's church are closed to her, it is unlikely that she will become enthusiastically involved in the adult church.

A friend of mine sent an unruly boy out to sit in the lobby during the service. This boy had come in on a Sunday school bus and didn't understand the concept of discipline in children's church. That afternoon, this boy and his family were killed in an apartment fire. My children's pastor friend wrote to me asking that I caution other children's church leaders. Do all you can to keep the children in a place where they can hear the good news. He now deals with every disruption in the back or side of his children's church service.

Children want discipline and loathe punishment. In Lois Le-Bar's 1952 book, *Children in the Bible School*, she writes, "Discipline is Needed and includes Instruction, Correction, and Encouragement."

Now isn't that N.I.C.E.? Children do need and want discipline. The discipline they are taught in church will spill over into every area of life. The Christian life is one of discipline. After all, self-discipline is a fruit of the Spirit.

Instruct the child in patient love. Let's have no finger-wagging, nagging teachers in children's church. Let him know what was done wrong and why it is important. Show the benefits of obedience as outlined in Scripture. Take this opportunity to train him up in the way he should go.

Correction is a process that turns the offender from bad to good. This may include a stiff lecture but always is laced with, and includes, prayer. Pray with the child and allow him to pray. Repentance is the act of turning from evil to do right.

Encouragement recognizes the worth of the child in your sight and God's. Let him know that you believe he can follow your rules. Encourage him to be a doer of the Word of God, not a hearer only.

Now here are some thoughts about discipline to keep in mind. Before you have a disruption:

• Decide never to use corporal punishment. Children must never be physically assaulted by anyone at church. Spanking, rough-housing, slapping, or dragging have no place in your children's church.

• Develop and reinforce simple rules. This lets them know your expectations and gives you a base for discussion when discipline becomes necessary.

• Remind them of your rules. Each Sunday you will want to begin your service with a reminder of your rules for church time. From time to time, without great fanfare, restate the rules. Repetition is the key to learning.

• Never brag on the consequences of disobedience. The minute you tell them what will happen if they break your rules, somebody will do it just to see if you are serious.

• Be positive. I tell the kids each week that they can obey the rules. Proverbs 16:21 says, "Pleasant words promote instruction." Be pleasant. Positive messages from the teacher throughout a class session can greatly improve overall behavior. You might say, "I like how Dave is sitting up straight and paying attention," or "I am glad that Jean is doing such a wonderful job obeying our rules."

• Determine right now to never embarrass a child in front of his peers. Would Jesus make fun of a child's mistakes? Would he disapprove of a child's expression of creativity because it is different from others? Would he mock another for all to enjoy? I think not. Treat children with the same respect you desire from them.

• Visit the home whenever possible. There is no substitute for a relationship with the child and her parents. A visit to the home will tell you much about the effects of lifestyle on behavior. You learn much about a child when seeing her room at home. Begin to understand her through her everyday environment.

When disruptive behavior is present:

• Change your activity. Perhaps you are the problem. If more than a couple of children are getting restless, shift gears and get them actively involved in the message. My mother says, "If the children are busy, they don't have time to be discipline problems." Mom ought to know. She has taught elementary school since I was a class clown in the third grade.

• Walk in the child's direction. A bit of eye contact and a step or two toward the child will many times cause a cease-fire without a single word uttered.

- Put your hand on the child's shoulder. Sometimes a hand gently placed on the shoulder will help a child with that temporary lack of self-control.

- Use the two-week rule. If a child disrupts your class two weeks in a row, then talk to his parents. You may discover a reason for this new behavior. (You may find out the parents are part of the problem.)

- Pray for the children who become disruptive. Pray that God will surround them with his peace and give you an extra dose of compassion.

- Provide the shadow. If a child becomes a continuing nuisance, assign an adult worker of the same gender to sit by him and help him to grow in self-control. When necessary, the "shadow" moves the child to the back of the room where he continues to teach, observe and assist the child.

- Switch seating. Never return a child to the same seat after you have talked and prayed with him. Seat her somewhere else in the room so that she may not be tempted by this regular audience. She will also be motivated to behave the next time she sits with her friends so that she might remain with them.

GAMES

I heard it said once or twice that a child's work is his play. Kids love games and learn valuable lessons for living from them.

I do not use games on a weekly basis. In our children's church, games are generally reserved for the post prayer time (if any exists). Games may begin after the final prayers are said. In effect, we close all serious times of meeting with God before we open the Bible Bowl.

These games are designed to reinforce both general and specific Bible knowledge, the latter having been taught during the preceding service.

A great percentage of the time, the games we use pit one half of the room against the other. Boys can compete against the girls, but we make this no requirement.

An effort is made to keep competition on a friendly Christlike level. We wish to have fun. There is no place in the church for highly competitive, Little League kinds of games. Here are some of the games we use:

TEDDY BEAR IN THE WASTEBASKET

A large trash container is placed on a table or the piano. A line of tape is placed on the floor about six feet away. Another line of tape is laid out somewhere in the rear of the room. (This game reflects the fact that I do not like to spend money.) Children answering a lesson-related question may throw a teddy bear from one of the lines. If Teddy falls into the basket, points are awarded to the appropriate team. More points are given for a basket from the line farthest from the wastebasket.

TIC-TAC-TOE

A representative from each team is designated to play the game. Team members answer questions to earn the right for their representative to place his mark on the board. Some people have created magnetic, flannel board or computerized versions of this. I use a dry-erasable marker board.

QUIZ DOWN

The children are divided into two teams. Each team stands in a single-file line at the front of the room. One by one they are asked questions. A correct answer allows the child to stay at the front of the line. An incorrect answer will send a child to the back of his line. He should have another opportunity to answer before the game is over.

You may also mark a line with tape on the floor. Every child who answers correctly takes a step over that line. The team having the most players standing over the tape line when the parents arrive wins.

THE RACE

There are a multitude of variations to this game. One is to stand two empty soda-pop bottles on a table. A funnel is placed in the mouth of each of them. For every correct team answer, a predetermined amount of liquid is poured into their bottle. The bottle which is filled first declares the winner.

WACKY OLYMPICS

"Strange" and "wonderful" are the key words for this type of game. One church had kids running to the back of the room, popping a balloon, pushing a toddler toy to the front, and hitting a buzzer pad before they could answer a question. Dream big and use those old toddler toys that are cluttering your closets at home.

MOTIVATION

Einstein once said, "Ninety-eight percent of education is motivation." I read that once and said to myself, "Hey, myself! This is absolutely true!" Discipline difficulties dissipate whenever I discover what motivates a particular child.

The big question comes immediately to mind: How can I motivate the kids so that they will want to participate in the children's church service? What is it that motivates children?

Before we jump off the deep end, before we tackle the tacky, before we dig into the world's largest banana split or give away the three-foot chocolate Easter rabbit, let us look at the purpose for motivating children.

I always approach motivation from an individual standpoint. A teacher once told me, "We don't teach lessons, we teach individuals." Every child is motivated differently.

Educators often talk about intrinsic and extrinsic motivation. Intrinsic refers to motivation from within. Extrinsic is from without.

The intrinsically motivated child has an enthusiastic desire to achieve. This personal momentum comes from within. She is a self-starter. She is a "gifted" student. This child needs no push from the teacher. She will memorize the Scripture, teach the story, and even volunteer for prayer.

A smart teacher will recognize the intrinsically motivated child and simply point her in the right direction. When growing through her elementary and high school years, my daughter Sarah was one of these. When assigned a project of any kind, Sarah desired to accomplish it as quickly and with as much perfection as possible. Mom and Dad did not have to push, plead, or threaten. This intrinsic motivation was reflected in her scholastic achievement.

When it came to household chores, however, this same wonderfully self-motivated daughter needed an extrinsic push. This brings an important point to mind. A child, or adult, can be extrinsically or intrinsically motivated at different times and for different reasons.

Extrinsic motivation is that power from the outside. It is the child that pushes the lawn mower; the mower wouldn't move without being pushed. And the child wouldn't push without the parents' threats of bodily harm or promise of allowance. And the parents wouldn't threaten and give money if they were not afraid of the neighbors' opinion. Everyone is motivated externally in this scenario.

In the children's church, extrinsic motivation takes on the guise of prizes. Star charts, candy bars, and free trips to local restaurants or amusement parks all serve as external motivations.

Even the serious, service-seeking children's pastor will have an occasional contest or big day. Contests can help bring in more children and control the ones you have. The key is not to let the contests control you.

My goal, however, is always to move children from the external to the internal to the eternal. A child may memorize a Scripture in order to win a prize. Once that Scripture finds its way from the child's head to his heart, a desire to learn more is planted. This child then learns Scripture even when there is no prize offered. Eventually he will apply those verses eternally as he gives his life to Jesus.

A girl in our church once brought twenty-seven visitors for a special outreach week. She bribed her friends with promises of puppets, prizes, and ice cream cones on the way home. The friends came and found a warm, fun place. They were internally motivated to return night after night. Some of those friends found Jesus in that crusade. They had moved from the external to the internal to the eternal.

The girl, after winning the visitor contest, said, "I started bringing kids 'cause I wanted the big prize. Then I saw some of my friends at the altar and just wanted to bring more."

You will find that boys and girls are motivated by many different things. Take time to discover what motivates the children you serve. Apply this knowledge as you plan future services.

The goal of motivation is to move them from the

- **External** to the
- **Internal** to the
- **Eternal**

children in family worship

I have stated that one of the purposes of a children's church is to prepare children for a meaningful transition into adult worship. Is children's church in a balanced service format enough? I hardly think so. Children need parental reinforcement and regular visits to the adult or family worship setting.

"Then little children were brought to Jesus for him to place his hands on them and pray for them. But the disciples rebuked those who brought them. Jesus said, 'Let the little children come to me, and do not hinder them, for the kingdom of heaven belongs to such as these'" (Matthew 19:13–14).

In many churches today, children are given no opportunity to worship, give, or respond to the pastor's preaching. The common practice that is sweeping our nation is parallel childcare. What I mean by this is that every time the doors of the church are opened for service, child care, (children's service or circus time), is provided.

We are, in practice, raising a generation of potential church dropouts. These children have never experienced a multigenerational worship service. They have not had opportunity to become enculturated to the adult worship mode. In my denomination alone, an alarming rate of almost 37 percent of these children will filter out of our back doors in their seventh and eighth grade years.

Yet pastors will stand and declare the success of the Sunday evening service. I heard one pastor excitedly proclaim, "We just couldn't get people out on Sunday nights until we started a Sunday evening children's church. Now we have the biggest crowds ever."

Perhaps it is a societal trend. Adults are looking for a country club church experience: pay their dues, claim their pews, and hear the news. Like the country club, the church hires others to take care of unwanted duties such as child care, maintenance, and cooperative service. In the country club you can attend when you feel like it, without obligation.

Let me challenge you to break from the Matthew 19:13 kind of church agenda. Refuse to accept the mistaken notion that the children would be better served somewhere out of sight and sound of their parents. This practice serves the adult adherents with no regard to the long-term effect on the spiritual development of the child.

Children need to experience family worship. Parents need to experience family worship. Scripture indicates God's desire to include children in worship and instruction:

> There was not a word of all that Moses had commanded that Joshua did not read to the whole assembly of Israel, including the women and children, and the aliens who lived among them (Joshua 8:35).

> All the men of Judah, with their wives and children and little ones, stood there before the LORD (2 Chronicles 20:13).

> And on that day they offered great sacrifices, rejoicing because God had given them great joy. The women and children also rejoiced. The sound of rejoicing in Jerusalem could be heard far away (Nehemiah 12:43).

> But when the chief priests and the teachers of the law saw the wonderful things he did and the children shouting in the temple area, "Hosanna to the Son of David," they were indig-

nant. "Do you hear what these children are saying?" they asked him. "Yes," replied Jesus, "have you never read, 'From the lips of children and infants you have ordained praise'?" (Matthew 21:15–16).

It is our task as children's ministry leaders to educate our constituency. Therefore, I urge you:

• Allow children to worship. Children want to worship God. They want to worship by Mom and Dad's side. Children need to witness the faithfulness of their parents as they give tithes and offerings, take notes on the pastor's sermon, and respond at the altar.

• Accommodate children in worship. Give children a place in your total church worship goals. The reason many children do not participate in so-called family worship services is that such services have not been designed for the entire family. They are simply adult services with children present. When children are not given a part in these services, parents become frustrated disciplinarians instead of intent worshipers.

• Assist children in worship. All ages should be encouraged to worship. Helps can be provided that will make children feel a part of your family service. God does inhabit the praises of his people. Point out that there is no age limit on worship set in Scripture, that everybody in the body of Christ should be included.

Thomas Trask wrote, "Worship is the act of giving honor, respect, and reverence to a Being who is worthy of the same. So real worship ought to mean continual conversion of thoughts, standards, and aims from a self-centered to a God-centered focus."[1]

Our aim in children's ministry is to assist children in this conversion. We, through our example, our relationships with God and the student, and our inclusion of children in a variety of worship experiences, can see this worship lifestyle emerge. Children need family worship experiences as much as they need children's church.

A child typically attends Sunday school and children's church on Sunday mornings. He is being trained in the way he should go. In Sunday school, doctrine is systematically presented using a variety of methods. In children's church, the gospel is presented in a worship format. Children give praise to God, learn and respond to a message, and participate up front. This is all geared to a child's level of understanding and provides peer reinforcement for positive spiritual growth.

As I have already said, our task is one of preparing children for sixty or seventy years of participation in adult worship. The kind of worship Thomas Trask writes about requires more than can be provided in the children's church setting. The family worship service completes the cycle of training that a child needs for healthy and continued involvement in corporate worship.

MAKING SERVICES CHILD-FRIENDLY

Your efforts to make this time child-friendly will strongly carry the message to parents that your church loves families. But remember these points in doing this:

• Don't do the same thing every week. For example, using even the most exciting puppets can become mundane and boring when overused.

• Do not talk down when addressing the children. Those in positions of authority in the family worship should treat children as part of the body. A voice may be softened without sounding phony or sing-songy. If pastors and other church leaders treat children with respect, it will be mirrored in the children's attitudes toward them.

• Involve children whenever and however you can. There is no surer way to interest the body of young believers than to place one of their friends in the limelight. (The children will sit up and take notice if only to watch their friend make a mistake.)

• Don't worry about perfection. Children will not do a perfect job every time they are up front. The wonder is that your congregation will overlook imperfection on a child's part. Parents and non-parents alike will sit on the edge of their seats rooting for a child. You can't go wrong when allowing a child to minister up front. People will enjoy it and the child who has had the opportunity will grow up with a leaning toward ministry. Here are some ways to develop a truly family worship service, accommodating the children:

PRAYER

• Boys and girls want to pray. It takes only a word of encouragement from the pulpit to include them. Many times they sit back and watch because the prayer time is perceived as an adult event. An invitation should be given verbally to the children. If they don't hear you say "boys and girls," chances are they will believe you are not speaking to them.

• When asking for prayer requests, include the children. Some churches keep a stack of prayer request cards in each pew. Children and adults are encouraged to fill them out and drop them in the offering bag as it passes. Treat every request sincerely. By doing so, you are training children in the importance of prayer. You will also, through this action, instill in children the reality of the verse, "Cast all your anxiety on him because he cares for you" (1 Peter 5:7).

• Encourage families to sit together and hold hands to pray. Part of our mission on earth is to strengthen the family. A bond of prayer is not easily broken.

• A child can be invited to offer prayer during any part of the service: upon its opening, during prayer request time (including prayer for the sick), for the offering, or at the service's conclusion.

• Children are marvelous prayer warriors. When inviting people down for prayer, ask if any children would like to pray for others. You will be surprised at the number of children who take this ministry seriously. Children come to Jesus with simple faith and great things happen.

SPECIAL SERVICES

• At least once a month your church should present missions. A short lesson or story will interest the children and serve to place importance on missions.

• Include children in the planning of special church days. For instance, children can participate in annual Christmas or Easter programs. They can play a big part in helping with the Sunday night kickoff of a kids' crusade or vacation Bible school.

• Many churches hold an occasional service run by the youth group. Teens lead in prayer, worship, receive the offering, and preach. Why not bring this down a step? With the supervisory assistance of Sunday school teachers, children can lead a service for your congregation several times a year.

SERMONS

• When I preach in an evening family service, I begin by giving the main points of my sermon. I then ask the children if they will help me remember these points. We repeat the points together, and as the sermon progresses I depend on the children to shout out the points from time to time so that we all remember where the sermon is headed and when it will be over.

• Keep sermons in the family worship service short and to the point. Good meat doesn't have to be surrounded by excessive entrees. Use storytelling skills to your advantage. Children and adults love to hear a good story.

• Illustrate the sermon whenever possible. Jesus used object lessons and other illustrative means to drive home deep spiritual thoughts. Your congregation will not only enjoy illustrated sermons, but they will retain and live the message that has been preached.

• Many pastors take a segment of the Sunday service to invite children up front for a talk. This little chat with the pastor helps children grow in love and appreciation for their pastor. A pastor who gives time to the children can expect reasonable attention from them at other times in the service.

• Perhaps the most radical concept is to allow children to actually preach or teach before the congregation. There are children that have a gift of teaching. These boys and girls love to share Bible knowledge with others. A child may explain one point of the sermon or give the whole sermon.

MUSIC AND WORSHIP

• Invite some children to join your worship team. Many churches have a team of three or four adults who lead in congregational worship. Including children on this team will immediately gain the attention of all children present.

• Many children take instrumental music lessons through either private teachers or public schools. The public schools will showcase these children in monthly PTA meetings and at local shopping malls. The church, too, should make a place for these kids. Schedule children who have played an instrument a year or longer. When they play in your evening service, younger children will be encouraged to begin study and to use this talent for the Lord.

DRAMA

• Puppets can present songs or skits. Adults as well as children enjoy puppet presentations. Puppets can bring a humorous angle to a message that may not be received in any other form of delivery.

• Once in a while a dramatic skit can serve to emphasize a spiritual truth. Allow children to take part in a drama troupe at your church. The whole family will enjoy skits of either a comedic or dramatic nature.

• Human video has become a very popular venue for children involved in ministry. Dramatizing a song in this way gives a large group of children opportunity to minister to their parents.

SCRIPTURES

• Invite a child to the pulpit to read the Scripture text for the evening's sermon. Many children have very good reading skills and would gladly participate in this way.

• A pastor I know opens his service each week with prayer. After prayer, he invites anyone, young or old, to share a meaningful verse of Scripture. Many children come ready to quote or read a passage to the entire congregation. This seems to be a fulfillment of 1 Corinthians 14:26 where it says, "What then shall we say, brothers? When you come together, every one has a hymn, or a word of instruction, a revelation, a tongue or an interpretation. All of these must be done for the strengthening of the church."

• A demonstration of Scripture knowledge can be presented by children in the evening service. Some pastors are taking a brief time during the service to ask children questions from the Bible. These little quiz times encourage all members present to sharpen their Bible knowledge.

OBJECT LESSONS

• An object lesson can be used to introduce the theme of the evening's sermon. This sermon can be presented by the pastor, Sunday school teacher, or an older child.

• When using object lessons in your sermon, invite a child or children up front to hold the objects. You can hold an object up yourself, but involving a child will capture the attention of all children present.

OTHER IDEAS

• Print a bulletin just for kids. It can include Bible quiz questions, puzzles, memory verses, word from the pastor, announcements, an outline of the sermon, and a place to take notes or draw pictures.

• Children can, under the direction of the regular ushers, serve in ushering. However, don't do this more than one Sunday a month; you want this kind of ministry to be a special opportunity.

• Give parents a list of questions to be discussed with their children after church. This will encourage both parents and children to pay more attention to what is being said from the pulpit.

• Churches with club ministries should encourage boys and girls to dress in uniform when helping in the evening service. There is no better way to promote an awareness in the congregation of the value of such programs. Seeing happy children in uniform serving God will make a lasting impression on people.

• Most pastors do not like to read announcements. Allow children to take part in announcement time. Have two or three children read them, add your seal of approval, and everybody will pay attention.

• Children can help operate equipment. In one church I noticed children in the sound booth. The church sound man was training children so that they could run sound for their morning children's church service.

I trust that you will begin to make your Sunday evening service a true family service. You will notice a difference in your congregation. Large or small, a church that includes all ages in a family service will begin to develop a family-friendly feeling, which will reach beyond your walls.

Children and parents will begin to enjoy worship together. As this happens, families will be stronger, response will be heartfelt, and a foundation will be laid for a future of God-centered believers who worship in spirit and in truth.

ALTERNATE PLANS TO THE FAMILY SERVICE

"But what if my senior pastor insists on my running an evening children's program?" You are a servant. At this juncture you can leave town or discover creative ways to make this evening program different from your morning Sunday school and church service.

Here are a few suggestions:

• Provide a kids' music time. This time can be spent in choir, age-level training, or even group instrumental or voice lessons.

• Some churches use Sunday evening as a time of in-depth doctrinal study. Each denomination has its own course of study for such classes.

• This is an ideal time to involve children in a Bible quiz program. Study, games, and quiz matches can fill this time with something worthwhile.

• Create a junior college of ministry training. Children can be trained in puppetry, clowning, prayer, drama, mime, and even equipment operation. Children who attend can be used in their ministries in the morning children's church, during Sunday school, or once a month in a special evening service for the whole family.

• Many slip into the mode of running a regular children's service. If you do this, be sure to develop segments and characters that differ from your morning service. Variety is the spice of life.

• Learning centers, games, crafts, and other reinforcing activities keep children moving through a time of Bible discovery. Variety and hands-on involvement are the keys to success.

Using one or a combination of these, you can build a quality evening program for children. Do all you can to impress upon leadership the need for corporate intergenerational worship times. If you end up running an evening as well as a morning program for the kids, smile and do your best for Jesus.

those fabulous volunteers

You will discover that a cutting-edge children's church cannot be developed without a faithful crew of volunteers. I am always on the lookout for kid-friendly lay people that can make a difference in my children's church. Here are some pointers I've discovered over the years in recruiting new volunteers for children's church and other ministries.

CAUTION!

The average church has a continuous need for workers. The pastor recruits from the pulpit on a regular basis. She speaks to heart and conscience until somebody, out of genuine concern, guilt, or frustration, finally volunteers. The pastor knows help is needed, the congregation knows help is needed, and the local child abuser knows help is needed. The church must do all it can to ensure the safety of those in its care. Every volunteer must fill out an application for ministry that includes a background check. That application should be processed and a file kept on each worker. This applies to every worker, teacher, coordinator, or helper that comes in contact with a minor.

RECRUIT FOR TOMORROW

Do not stop recruiting when every position is filled. Recruitment of leaders should be constant. Recruit for the future. Today there may be ten children in your children's church. Next year at this time there will be twenty-five. A growing church will have need of new leaders on a regular basis. Create entry level positions for new recruits while they are in training.

DO NOT RECRUIT TEACHERS

Most pastors are looking for teachers. Most people do not think they can teach. So most churches have an excess number of people pew warming while the need remains for help in the children's church or Sunday school. Begin recruiting people into "entry level" positions. Recruit craft coordinators, snack helpers, role takers, storytellers, audio-visual technicians, hall monitors, greeters, grandparents, music leaders, and other teaching assistants. People want to know that they are part of a team and as such, will not be stuck in a classroom alone with the children.

GIVE THEM THE PERSONAL TOUCH

Everyone likes to feel that they are needed. Rarely does anyone take personally an appeal for help from the pulpit. "The pastor must be talking to someone else." Do not rely on announcements from the pulpit or pleas placed in the church mailer. Take your recruiting to the homes and lives of individuals. It is hard to say no when the question is being posed face to face.

MAKE RECRUITING A SPIRITUAL ACT

Pray to the Lord of the harvest! He will send laborers. When recruiting an individual, include God in the process. NO, do not use Scripture or quote some new revelation from on high to browbeat or make a potential volunteer feel guilty.

Encourage the prospective worker to pray for God's will in this matter. You may need a sound technician in children's church, but you want God's will to be accomplished as that person finds his or her place of ministry. Everyone should be involved somewhere in the work of ministry.

Recruiting is the first step in matching a person and his gifts with a ministry. Give him a week to pray about the decision and let him know at the end of that week you will call and discuss where God would place him in ministry. At the end of that week when the saint says "yes," have him fill out your volunteer application and enroll him in a basic course of training. Should he say, "no," find out where he feels he fits in ministry in the church. In this way, I have recruited many people for areas of ministry other than my children's church.

REQUIRE REGULAR CHECK-UPS

A star athlete must keep in training. The coach doesn't just set him on the field and leave him to flounder without direction. Your volunteers need a regular touch from you. It is not enough to recruit a person and hope they will survive. Set up a system of visitation in which you will spend time with each volunteer on a regular basis. Love the volunteers and they will love you.

One other thing: volunteers need clearly defined duties. Keep in mind that these people are not paid to run your children's church. Any way you can facilitate their ministry by keeping it simple and enjoyable will be appreciated.

CHILDREN'S CHURCH VOLUNTEER GUIDELINES

You have just volunteered to help in children's church. This ministry will impact boys, girls and their families for years to come. Here are some practical guidelines to assist you in doing the best job you can for the glory of God.

THE SERVICE: General Guidelines

1. Cleanliness is next to godliness. Brush your teeth, comb your hair, use deodorant, wear clean clothes. You are representing Jesus. Look and smell your best for him. The children and other leaders will appreciate this.

2. Prayer changes things. Pray for God's anointing on our service, on the other workers, on your portion of the program and on the other

services at church. Pray for the kids. Our desire is that God would do something new in each child each week.

3. Preparation pays big time. Even the person with the smallest part must prepare.

4. Remember Colossians 3:23–24. "Whatever you do, work at it with all your heart, as working for the Lord, not for men, since you know that you will receive an inheritance from the Lord as a reward. It is the Lord Christ you are serving."

5. Sunday school is important. All visuals must be prepared and in place prior to the Sunday school hour. Each worker in the children's church attends a Sunday school class. We do not spend that hour preparing for children's church.

6. Always treat children with respect. Jesus said, "...I tell you the truth, whatever you did for one of the least of these brothers of mine, you did for me" (Matthew 25:40). Your speech should always lift children to Jesus. Encourage each child. Learn and use names with respect.

7. Children want to serve. Whenever possible, involve children in your portion of the service. Have them hold objects, dramatize stories, or run the technology. This, after all, is *children's* church. (Pay attention to children that are used in ministry by the other workers. We want to involve as many different boys and girls as possible in each service each week.)

8. Sit with the children. Workers are to be part of the service. Never stand in the back of the room or congregate in small groups away from the kids.

9. Your life is an example. Workers must be involved in the entire service. Your worship, participation, and following of the rules (No Walk, No Talk), set an example to the children.

10. Compliment children for positive behavior (Proverbs 16:21). Some call this positive reinforcement. Children are motivated by adults and teens who notice their good deeds and recognize them.

11. Remember the theme. Each service follows or teaches a specific theme. Keep the theme in mind and weave it into any lesson you might be called upon to present.

12. The Rule Of Three will be enforced. No worker will have one-on-one contact with a child apart from the group. You do not take a child alone into the hallway or restrooms. You do not spend time privately with any child either on or off the church grounds. Always walk in threes or more. Spending time with several children is permitted. The Rule Of Three states, "There will never be less than three people in any given situation. This can be two workers and one child, or one worker and two children."

THE SERVICE: Specific Guidelines

Sound

1. Turn on system.
2. All microphones will be checked prior to the children entering the room.
3. Play slow, worshipful music as children enter the room.
4. Pay attention to the platform area at all times.
5. Do not become involved in conversation with others at the sound booth.
6. Ensure that all CDs, DVDs, or MP3s are in the proper order and ready for the service.
7. Ensure that microphone chords are untangled and rolled neatly next to their stands.
8. Put away any extra equipment used at conclusion of the service.
9. Play the fast, fun children's music as children exit.
10. Turn off system after children have departed.

Master of Ceremonies

1. Gather workers for prayer prior to opening the service. Discuss order of service, theme, and encourage workers as you pray.
2. Open service in a positive way. Include theme, meet with each other and meet with God, the two rules (No Walk, No Talk), and pray.
3. Tie each segment together with emphasis on the theme of the day. There should be no dead time between segments. Fill time with teaching and theme reinforcement until the next worker is ready to start his or her lesson.
4. You are the authority in the room. The buck stops with you.
5. Remind children of the rules occasionally throughout the service.
6. Be open to the move of God. If worship needs to last longer, keep it going. If you feel the Spirit leading into a special prayer time, do it!
7. Stand at side or back when not on stage and monitor all activity. If children are not into a specific part of the service, you have the authority to signal the worker to close his portion.
8. Be ready to fill time at the end of the service with an extra lesson or Bible quiz game that will reinforce the theme of the day.
9. Be polite to any and all visitors to the service. Parents may sit with their children, but others should be encouraged to sit near the back.

Worship

1. This is a service. Treat it as such. We are not playing at worship.
2. Pay attention to the children and be sensitive to the Holy Spirit.

3. Begin with two or three fast/action choruses. Conclude with a couple of slower songs.

4. Do not feel rushed. Let God move in and among the children.

5. Use children to assist in worship leading. (Pay attention to children that are used by the other workers. We want to involve as many different boys and girls as possible in each service each week.)

6. Use the microphone. It helps those in the back.

7. Praise breaks, testimonies, or times of silence are recommended.

8. Use familiar and age-appropriate songs. Introduce no more than one new song each week.

9. Worship is the key to success in the continuation of our children's service. When children enter into worship, discipline problems fade, and hearts become receptive to the living God.

10. Worship always flows into a time of prayer for the sick.

Giving

1. Prayer for the sick will be conducted as a transition between worship and giving. If this is not led by the worship leader or MC of the day, the responsibility falls on you. Praying one for another is an incredibly intimate way of giving to the Lord.

2. Missions will be promoted during giving time on the fourth Sunday of each month.

3. You are to prepare some kind of lesson concerning giving of tithes, offerings, time, or talents. This can be an object lesson, story, costumed character, or other illustration. (No lectures allowed!)

4. Involve children in the giving lesson. (Pay attention to children that are used by the other workers. We want to involve as many different boys and girls as possible in each service each week.)

5. Choose children to be ushers prior to the opening of the service. These can be any age and will be instructed to be ready at the offering time.
6. Ensure that offering receptacles are in place and ready to be used prior to the opening of the service.
7. All offering is taken to the back of the room, placed in the accounting bag, and turned into the church office or wherever your pastor directs. Always pray for the offering and those who participate.
8. Use the microphone when teaching the children.

Crowd Control

1. You may sit with the children, but be ready to move at any time.
2. Pay attention to the children around you. The happenings on the platform are supposed to be interesting, but do not require your undivided attention.
3. You are here to help every child have a positive experience in church. A disruptive child can ruin church for those around him.
4. Every child has occasional lapses in self control. Treat the disruptive child with respect.
5. When any child misbehaves, follow the simple guidelines listed below.
   a. Never physically hurt a child. No corporal punishment will be tolerated.
   b. Handle all difficulties quietly and efficiently.
   c. Treat the child as an individual created in the image of God.
   d. A gentle touch on the shoulder may be all that is needed to halt a disruption.
   e. Eye contact with the child may be enough to bring peace.

f. You may need to move the child or make room to sit by him.

g. If a child needs to be disciplined, take her to the back of the room and assist her in gaining some self control. Always follow your church's discipline policy.

Scripture Verse

1. The same verse is used for all children's church services in a given month.
2. Do not use the same method for teaching a verse two weeks in a row.
3. Recite the verse once or twice for the children.
4. Introduce your visual method.
5. Have children repeat the verse two to five times as your method is used.
6. Before taking your seat, say the verse together one last time. Unity is far greater than increased volume.
7. Keep the Scripture time brief and exciting. The Bible must always be presented as the most exciting book ever written. Remember, God inspired the Bible.
8. Involve the children in teaching, holding visuals or sorting words. (Pay attention to children that are used by the other workers. We want to involve as many different boys and girls as possible in each service each week.)

Bible Story

1. Pray for creative ways to teach the story. Most children have heard these stories before. You must make it new and interesting to them.
2. Use children to help teach, act out, or hold visuals for the story. (Pay attention to children that are used by the other

workers. We want to involve as many different boys and girls as possible in each service each week.)

3. Keep the Bible story time brief and exciting. The Bible must always be presented as the most exciting book ever written. Remember, God inspired the Bible.

4. Emphasize the theme of the day as it relates to the story. Children need to learn the message behind each story as well as the facts.

5. Whenever possible use an open Bible as you tell the story.

6. Practice your storytelling technique. The story should stand on its own if your visuals fail.

7. Wherever possible recreate the story visually. It doesn't have to cost money or be elaborate to be effective.

Care Ministers

1. You are a representative of Christ.

2. Always smile and treat the contact with respect.

3. Fill out the card as completely as possible. We need as much information as we can get.

4. If the child is a visitor, welcome him, fill out card, and invite him to return.

5. Be friendly.

6. If the child has just accepted Christ as Savior, talk with him, pray with him, fill out card, and encourage him to read the Bible and pray each day. If he needs a Bible, give him one.

7. Copy the child's name and number on a piece of paper for your records.

8. Pray for that child and call him on the phone at least once during the week.

WE LOVE KIDS! LET'S SHOW IT!

a final word or two

Your children's church, is it cutting edge? Is it a circus or a service? Is it a Sunday morning snack session or a banquet table where children taste and see that the Lord is good?

Since the day that God placed me in a children's church, I have wanted to be the best I can be. My desire has been to glorify God through every object lesson, snack time, and puppet spectacular. In every lesson I present, I want the children to be directed to the cross, and the Christ of that cross.

Gruber as Zerubbabel the Clown

There have been times of discouragement. There have been times of sorrow and of laughter. There have been times of wonderful blessing and dismal failure.

Through it all, God has kept this desire at the forefront of my mind: I can always improve what I am doing. God has always been at my side granting me strength and wisdom and creativity. This same marvelous Savior will be at your side.

There is never an excuse for mediocrity in ministry to children. God has placed you in a children's church. That children's church can be a valid worship experience. You can have fabulous props, creative lessons, and powerful altar services.

Go to seminars. Learn all you can about ministry to and through children. Apply those things that will work in your church setting. Adapt or file those things that will not.

But with all the evaluation and sharpening of tools, never forget that God has entrusted you with this task. Your children's church belongs to Jesus. Every week he walks the aisle. He loves the disruptive child. He hugs the lonely child. He desires the worship of every child. He longs to commune in prayer with every boy, girl, and volunteer.

Remember Jesus in your preparation and presentation. That sounds silly, doesn't it? How could you forget Jesus? This is church. Do like Ezra of old. He "devoted himself to the study and observance of the Law of the LORD, and to teaching its decrees and laws in Israel" (Ezra 7:10).

If you have been operating a Sunday morning circus, I pray that the words that you have read will open doors of possibility. You can attain a balance of worship, giving, preaching, and prayer.

Never settle for a circus again. Each week you should strive to prepare children for the fabulous future of adult worship. Each week, your service can be training children for a productive life of servanthood.

Become a cutting-edge leader with a cutting-edge children's church. This service for children will be: relational, age-level appropriate, inclusive, spiritual, and exciting.

It will be relational in that you and your team will build relationships with children and their parents. We know that all ministry is relational and your lesson material will have greater impact in the lives of those who know you as pastor and friend.

It will be age-level appropriate. Children will experience lessons and hands-on ministry that challenges them at whatever age they are. Your church time will inspire spiritual growth in the children you serve.

It will be inclusive. A parent once told me that her sixth grader was sitting in the car crying. The girl did not want to come into the church because while visiting the two weeks prior, she was not welcomed by her peers. Every child wants to be wanted. Create an atmosphere of unconditional love and acceptance.

It will be spiritual. Children will meet God in your children's church. They will be elevated into his presence through worship, education and experience. They will encounter God at the altar of response.

It will be exciting. Each week, children will be thrilled to step into your service because they will recognize that Jesus is there.

One day, when you stand before Jesus, He will say, "I was thirsty and you pushed the button on the water fountain. I was disruptive and you took the time to discipline me. I needed an outlet for my gift of teaching and you allowed me to stand and serve my friends as one of your helpers. I needed to spend time with the Father and you gave it to me in the children's church."

You will say, "Lord, when did I do all of these things?"

And the King will answer, "Whatever you did for, to, and with the boys and girls of your children's church, you have done for, to, and with me."

Your cutting-edge children's church will be the overflow of your cutting-edge relationship with Jesus. Your planning, practice and presentations will be empowered by a God who loves the kids more than you do and wants you to succeed more than you can imagine.

appendix a: the gruber method

Many people have asked me over the years, "How does the balance look when fit into an actual children's church order of service?" I have designed an answer on the page below.

- Worship
    - ✓ Children enter—play slow, worshipful music while assisting children in taking their seats.
    - ✓ Opening—rules, prayer, and introduction of theme.
    - ✓ Songs—including a couple of fast songs, a couple of slow songs, and testimonies.
    - ✓ Prayer for special needs.
- Giving
    - ✓ Teaching on giving—utilizing a variety of methods, giving of time, tithe, and talents is taught regularly.
    - ✓ Offering is received.
    - ✓ A child or children minister.
- Preaching
    - ✓ Scripture verse.
    - ✓ Bible story.
    - ✓ Reinforcing lessons.
    - ✓ Final message leading into prayer time.
- Prayer
    - ✓ Response time held every week.
    - ✓ 10–20 minutes before estimated time of departure.
    - ✓ Utilize a variety of methodologies.

✓ If time permits, an extra lesson or two follows prayer reinforcing the theme of the day.
✓ Dismissal—play fun, fast music.

appendix b: the griz method

My friend Brian Grizwold has served as a children's pastor for over twenty-five years. He incorporates the four parts of a balanced service within his own unique outline for children's church. Each part of his service order begins with the letter "P" and has hand motions to assist children in remembering. Here is my interpretation of that service order:

• Pray—Folded hands—Pastor Griz talks to his kids in a calm, reassuring voice. He pauses before the last word of each phrase allowing them to fill it in. "We fold our hands to pray. We close our eyes. We bow our heads. We talk to God."

• Pledge—Hand over the heart—At this time pledge is made to the American flag with a brief explanation thanking God for the freedom we enjoy in this country.

• Pause—Hands open like a book in front of the body—A sword drill using the key Scripture of the day is held. The Scripture is read several times. Pastor Griz then tells the children to answer these three questions: "What does it say? What does it mean? What do you believe God is saying to you?" He then has several children finish this sentence: "I believe God is saying…" In this way, children begin to think about the Scripture and apply it to their lives.

• Play—Body is turned sideways with arms extended making an Egyptian-style "Z" form with one arm above and other below—A short game is played. Pastor Griz uses any game that works. It does not have to have anything to do with the lesson. He says, "Just make it fun!"

• Praise—Arms and open palms extended towards heaven—The worship band comes and plays a couple of fast songs and a couple of slow songs. Children are encouraged to worship God at this time with song and testimonies.

• Pay—Hands out with thumb and forefingers rubbing—A teaching on the importance of giving tithes and/or offerings is given at this time in the service. Pastor Griz wants every child to know that giving is important.

• Preach—Right arm upward with pointer finger extended—An object sermon is delivered in kid language and in accordance with the theme of the day. This always culminates with a response time.

• Pray—Hands folded—everyone is encouraged to spend some time in fellowship with God.

Pastor Griz says, "I assign each segment to a different worker. In this way, nobody is given an overload of work to do on any given Sunday."

appendix c: where is Jesus in your children's church?

Allow me to begin with a familiar Bible story. It is that time toward the end of Samson's judging days. Delilah has discovered his secret, cut his hair and called in the Philistines.

> Then she called, "Samson, the Philistines are upon you!" He awoke from his sleep and thought, "I'll go out as before and shake myself free." But he did not know that the LORD had left him (Judges 16:20).

I propose to you today that in many of our children's churches, Jesus has been chiseled down to a flannel-graph figure or curriculum point of interest. It is God's desire to work in and through every leader and helper in every service. He wishes to enter your children's church with the fresh anointing of his Holy Spirit. He desires to be part of the program, not just another point of interest on your Bible study charts.

The wise men asked, "Where is the one who was born king of the Jews?" Children are asking this question of children's church leaders today. Where is the real Jesus? Where is Jesus in your children's church?

Boys and girls are tired of leaders who plod through powerless sessions doing their time until pastor finds another. Kids want and need to experience the power of God in every service.

When my son Tim was two years old, we produced an Easter musical at our church. I arrived early to assist with make-up. The man playing the part of Jesus came out in full make-up and costume and talked with my family for a few minutes. As he left and the door swung closed behind him, Tim asked, "Is Jesus coming back?"

Good question, Tim! Is Jesus coming back? Boys and girls, young and old are wondering the same thing. Where is Jesus in your children's church? Without a vision and the power of God behind that vision, the children's church perishes!

Jesus can be found through three things in our children's church:
1. Well-prepared teachers
   a. Found in daily study of God's Word
   b. Found in godly curriculum
   c. Found in steady training to better their ministry
2. Well-presented lessons
   a. Message is all important
   b. Meditate on God's Word and curriculum
   c. Methodology that appeals to your audience
3. Well-prayed foundation which includes prayer for
   a. Students
   b. Pastors
   c. Anointing
   d. Ministry

Where is Jesus in your children's church?
- He's in the tear-stained cheeks of that nine-year-old who gives her life to the Lord next to an old metal folding chair.

- He's in the glory felt when sixth graders pray one for another and feel God's living presence.
- He's in the back of the room as a child hugs a leader and says, *I love you.*
- He's in the hallway as you push the button on that drinking fountain for a little one who cannot reach.
- He's in your patience as you minister lovingly to that foul-mouthed, dirty-nosed bus kid.

Samson was caught sleeping at the enemies' barber shop. He didn't even know the Lord was absent. Don't be caught sleeping. We live in a day and age when children need the Lord. You can be the inspiration that your church needs to pray in the return of Jesus in your children's church. Where is Jesus in your children's church? You tell me!

notes

Chapter 1: How Gruber Got into Children's Church

1. Reggie McNeal, *A Work of Heart: Understanding How God Shapes Spiritual Leaders.* (San Francisco: Jossey-Bass, 2000), 150.

2. C.H. Spurgeon, *Come Ye Children.* (Pasadena, Texas: Pilgrim Publications, 1975), 30.

3. Barna, George. *Transforming Children into Spiritual Champions.* (Ventura, California: Regal Books, 2003), 23.

4. Wideman, Jim. *Children's Ministry Leadership.* (Loveland, CO: Group Publishing, 2003), 27.

Chapter 3: From a Circus to a Service

1. Bob Hahn. "Children's Church, A Circus Without A Purpose?" *Small Steps.* Volume 1, Issue No. 2. (Champaign, IL: Don McGarvey Publishing, 1980).

2. Ibid.

Chapter 12: Children in Family Worship

1. Thomas E. Trask, "The Pastor and Congregational Services," in *And He Gave Pastors: Pastoral Theology in Action*, ed. Thomas F. Zimmerman (Springfield, MO: Gospel Publishing Housc, 1979), 282.

CPSIA information can be obtained at www.ICGtesting.com
Printed in the USA
BVOW080155070812

297242BV00005B/1/P